We Believe Series

Edward England, who inspired the *I Believe Series* published by Hodder and Stoughton, is the General Editor of this *We Believe Series* published by Marshall Morgan and Scott. The earlier series, edited by Canon Michael Green, was concerned with the theology of our faith. In each volume of this new series twelve or so contributors will make personal statements of faith, written from daily experience. The titles will include *We Believe in Healing, We Believe in Marriage, We Believe in Mission* and *We Believe in Guidance.*

While Edward England is General Editor of the series, each volume will have its own individual editors. *We Believe in Prayer* has been edited by Clifford Fryer, minister of a Baptist church in the seaside resort of Ilfracombe.

We Believe in Prayer

Edited by
Clifford Fryer

Marshalls

Marshalls Paperbacks
Marshall Morgan & Scott
3 Beggarwood Lane, Basingstoke, Hants, RG23 7LP, UK

Copyright © 1985 by Clifford Fryer

First published by Marshall Morgan & Scott Ltd

Unless otherwise mentioned, all Scripture quotations are taken
from the New International Version (NIV).

British Library CIP data

We believe in prayer.—(We believe series)
  1. Prayer
  I. Fryer, Clifford
248.3'2   BV210.2

  ISBN 0-551-01253-6

Typeset by Brian Robinson, North Marston, Bucks.
Printed in Great Britain by
Anchor Brendon Ltd, Tiptree, Essex.

To all who have troubled to pray for me
and thus helped me more than they can ever know.

'I kneel before the Father, from whom his whole
family in heaven and on earth derives its name.'

Paul

Contents

Introduction
The World's Greatest Miracle

I sit in my chair. I do not lift a finger. I do not even raise my voice. Yet something is changed around the other side of the world. Impossible? Yes. I pray – and the impossible happens.

I met God today. I spoke to him for half an hour. Don't send for the men in the white coats. It happened when I prayed. Is this not the world's greatest miracle? A little speck in the universe like me can speak to the eternal God: the Maker of heaven and earth.

This is not only true for me. All the contributors in this book testify to this greatest of all miracles. We are all very ordinary people. Our names are not likely to go down in the annals of world history (or even church history) but they are written in heaven. Nobody claims to be a prayer expert, but many lessons are recorded here which we trust will help your prayer life and encourage you to pray in faith in whatever situation you find yourself.

Come and join us in our many experiences. Our stories testify to a simple truth: *prayer works.*

Clifford Fryer

Malcolm Widdecombe

Prayer: The Nitty Gritty

Born 1937 in Gibraltar, where parents were with Ministry of Defence. Born again December 1955 at New Year House Party at Capernwray Hall.

1957–1962 attended Tyndale Hall Theological College, Bristol (which he refers to as his visit to purgatory, but secretly enjoyed it very much).

Served first curacy at Holy Trinity, Bristol.

1965 began second curacy at St Luke's, Barton Hill, Bristol, but with special responsibility for the pastoral ministry at SS Philip and Jacob Church, known as Pip'n'Jay for a trial period of three years.

1967 Priest-in-Charge of Pip'n'Jay.

1974 appointed Vicar of Pip'n'Jay. Pip'n'Jay has seen an increase of giving away to work outside its parish from £187 in 1964 to over £70,000 in 1983.

1974–1981 Co-leader with Denis Clark of Intercessors for Britain.

Since 1979 Rural Dean of Bristol City Deanery.

Mr Widdecombe has travelled extensively in this country and abroad, ministering on the subjects of stewardship, renewal and prayer.

He is married to Meryl, and they have Sean (sixteen), Roger (fourteen), Fiona (ten), Joab (five), Snowy (two and a half), the last two being the dog and cat respectively.

Dr Billy Graham has said, 'Jesus was one of the busiest men who ever lived, yet look at the time he spent in prayer.' The Bible tells us that we are to follow in his steps.

Every Christian knows that praying is something he ought to do, and most Christians go through life condemning themselves for not doing it enough. Ministers of the gospel are probably the worst culprits in this respect. The historic denominations become more and more bureaucratic. Members of their committees dream up more questionnaires. They draw up more strategy papers. They institute more working parties. They call up more clergy conferences. All these, of course, are with the splendid intention of helping the minister in his job, but usually result in wasting an inordinate amount of his time. He will conscientiously try to answer some of them, read some of them, attend others, and probably do too much. It all adds to the pressure of the day to day running of his own church, with administration, visitation, sermon preparation, and endless local committees. Something has to go. It is usually prayer. And John Wesley saying he had so much to do that he just had to spend two hours each day in prayer, does not help at all. It only adds to the sense of condemnation. J. Montgomery, the hymn writer said:

> Prayer is the Christian's vital breath,
> The Christian's native air.

Many Christians, laymen and ministers alike, struggling with the fast pace of twentieth-century life, admit to being very much out of breath.

Mission England in the summer of 1984 with the return to this country of Dr Billy Graham reminded us yet again of the importance of prayer. Dr Graham's secret of successful evangelism is threefold – prayer, prayer, and prayer. However, it is not only mass evangelism that depends on prayer for its success. The mission's Prayer Triplets scheme and the Operation Andrew Prayer Cards clearly demonstrated the importance of prayer in personal evangelism. All this we know – from our Lord's example, from the exhortation of Christian leaders past and present and even from our own personal experience. Why then is prayer the one aspect of our Christian walk that is the first to get neglected? The pat answer is to say it is because the devil doesn't like it when Christians pray and therefore he does all he can to frustrate them. Pat answer or no, it is the truth. We sing *'On the victory side'* but suffer too many defeats where prayer is concerned. I do not pretend to have all the answers, easy or otherwise; nor do I pretend to be a super-saint who has his prayer life buttoned up. Over the years the Lord has been very patient with this very rebellious and ill-disciplined servant. Not everything that follows will help everybody, but if just something rings a bell with someone, then with God's help we shall be able to chalk up a victory or two against the enemy of our souls.

The Sound Barrier

If the prayer meeting is the cinderella of church meetings, and if personal prayer is the most neglected part of our christian experience, it is because of what we Christians have done to prayer. I believe we have made it frightening, difficult, sometimes embarrassing and usually dead boring. Prayer is meant to be encouraging, easy, exciting and an exercise of common sense.

In the same way that I have believed in God for as long as I can remember, I have also believed in prayer. Gran, who lived with us during the War, encouraged me to pray. Usually it was a few petitions of the 'Bless Mummy, bless me' variety. All the people connected with home and school

14

got an honourable mention, including the cat (in the Widdecombe household cats = people). These prayers were made in bed before dropping off to sleep. I had no doubt at all that Someone heard.

In Prep School the pressure of unpleasant senior boys (who were all of twelve years old), a fiery headmaster, William Jameson (whom I feared and deeply loved), organised games, and end of term exams, lent urgency to my prayers which became a life line for my survival. School prayers I enjoyed, except for Fridays when the whole school had choir practice. Both at Prep School and Monkton Combe Senior School, most pupils enjoyed morning prayers and school chapel and looked forward to them.

Monkton Combe is a Christian School. I count it one of the great privileges of my life that my parents sent me there. I had been a day bug at the Prep, but I was a boarder at the Senior School.

The first night in the dormitory was something that I viewed with trepidation. In the event, the house prefect in charge of us explained that a bell would ring. This, he said, was for silence time. No one was to move about or talk. It was for those boys who wanted to read their Bibles and pray. I was quite delighted, then surprised as one after another the majority of the boys knelt beside their beds for prayer. I had always prayed in bed and associated kneeling with A. A. Milne's *'Little Boy Kneels at the Foot of the Bed'* – and thought it somewhat cissy. The house prefect also knelt down. He was a massive first fifteen rugby forward. I followed suit. I spent most of my time at Monkton doing just that, where Christian things were concerned. And it was not just playing 'copy-cat' either. I really did enjoy the Chapel, the Christian Union, and various voluntary Bible Studies. The fact that I wanted to serve and please God probably saved me from two prayer meeting disasters. One nearly scared the living daylights out of me, and the other made me curl up with humiliation.

The first occasion was a prayer meeting that I attended when still quite a junior. At that time I had never prayed

15

aloud at a prayer meeting, although I had attended many. This one was different. We were placed in a circle and informed that we were going to pray around. The prayers began and as my turn came nearer, I felt paralysed and my mind went a complete blank. I have a recurring nightmare of having to go on stage without the slightest knowledge of my lines. In a way it was a little like that. The boy next to me finished his prayer, and I died. Thankfully my decease was not for long. After thirty seconds of electric silence the boy on the other side of me began to pray.

I vowed never to go to a prayer meeting again. Others have made that vow and unfortunately kept it. A leader should always make sure that all the members of his prayer group are accustomed to praying aloud before starting a prayer 'round'. We often pray around the group at Pip'n'Jay, but always make sure it is possible for someone to opt out if they wish. An instruction like, 'If you don't wish to pray, please tap the person next to you on the shoulder', is effective enough and every newcomer or inexperienced Christian can then relax. A prayer meeting is not meant to frighten but to encourage.

Every Christian has to get through the sound barrier – the sound of his own voice in prayer in front of others. As a junior room officer at a teenager houseparty at Capernwray Hall, I observed a group of thirteen to fourteen year olds come through that barrier. There were about twelve boys in the room. Every morning Tony Gill, one of the houseparty leaders, and I organised a short prayer time for them before breakfast. Tony gave a Bible study lasting about five minutes. Then he introduced a prayer time. He invited the lads to pray a one sentence prayer about anything at all, but he stressed they were only to pray if they really wanted to. To help them he gave one or two examples of the sort of prayer that they could use. Then we prayed. He said a one sentence prayer. I said a one sentence prayer. We waited. The first morning we waited for a minute and then Tony closed. The second day two of the boys had a go, including one who prayed, 'Please help the kitchen staff in their struggle to feed us.' That lad prayed the same prayer every morning for the remainder of the week. Being the boy with the largest girth it doubtless came from his heart.

By the end of that week all the boys had prayed. Most of them had progressed from one sentence prayers to paragraphs. But they didn't get as far as chapters, thank God. Often a prayer meeting is killed stone dead by a verbose saint who cannot seem to stop his prayer. John Wesley tells of a man who in the first moments of his prayer prayed him into a good state of mind, but went on to pray for so long, that he prayed him right out of it again. I heard another preacher say that when a person prayed for five minutes he prayed with them; if the prayer continued a further five minutes he prayed for them; but should the prayer continue longer he began to positively pray against them. There is a place for lengthy, corporate intercession, but only where all members of the group have met for this purpose. It must also only take place where all members have long since been delivered from the mistake of confusing prayer with preaching. At Pip'n'Jay prayer meetings we sometimes limit one session to one sentence prayers only and we bar commas and semicolons. It can be very refreshing and nearly always encourages the less experienced to have a go. Another way to break the sound barrier is to write a short prayer on a piece of paper beforehand. At a suitable point in the meeting the prayer can be read out. A sympathetic group leader will encourage this, so that it becomes natural and no one thinks it odd. I reckon that one only needs to do this twice, before being able to manage a one sentence unscripted prayer without any trouble at all.

My second near disaster was at a prayer meeting held at school when I was about fifteen or sixteen. I had crashed through the sound barrier and had become quite wordy in my prayers. Pride always comes before a fall. I was praying for the Prime Minister (they need it more than most) and I got his name wrong, muddling him with the Home Secretary or some other member of the Cabinet. Almost immediately I realised my mistake. I finished my prayer

17

with the statutory 'Amen' and looked up. Two of the group were having a quiet laugh with each other over my gaffe. Again I wanted to die, and I certainly avoided that particular prayer group for the rest of term.

Prayer group leaders need to be sympathetic in managing their group. No one must be laughed at – though laughed with, certainly. If only someone had come to me afterwards and said, 'Doesn't matter a bit about muddling names. God knows who you meant. And thanks for your prayer. We need to pray more for bods in Government.' I hope our prayer group leaders at Pip'n'Jay would say something like that. All Christians are self-conscious, especially British Christians, who are more reserved than most. New Christians in particular need special care. The prayer meeting is meant to encourage and aid new spiritual growth. It is not meant to embarrass or stunt new life.

Prayer for Souls and Provision
In my last year at school a friend of mine, Tony Bush (now a farmer, member of General Synod, and recently Director of Mission England in the South West) accompanied me to a houseparty at Capernwray Hall. It is a long story. The short of it is I was converted. The God I had believed in for so long, and even loved, now became my personal Lord and Saviour. The great teaching emphasis at Capernwray is that each Christian is a soul winner.

For some time before my conversion I had guessed that God wanted me to be a minister. And I had viewed being a minister as first and foremost being a soul winner. This was because of the dynamic ministry of our school chaplain, the Rev Dudley Clarke. He had attended the Billy Graham Harringay Crusade, returned to school and put the senior Bible Study group through the crusade's counselling course. He was subsequently song leader at the Southampton Crusade led by Major Bill Batt. The latter, along with the Rev Dick Rees and other leading evangelists were frequent visitors to school chapel and conducted missions among us. Now that I was a Christian, I wanted to save souls. But how?

In those days there were very few opportunities for an eighteen year old to preach. It would have to be on the personal level. What happened was almost Prayer Triplets, though we didn't call it that.

Three of us got together and covenanted to pray for a week for three other boys in school. We agreed that at the end of that week we would each speak to our 'target' about his soul. Then we would report back to one another for a further time of prayer together. Each day we prayed for the three boys. I cannot say that it worked each time, because there is such a thing as free will but by the end of term more than a hundred boys had either come to Christ or made a real re-commitment of their lives to him. Each week when we met for 'Reports' the excitement grew. Not one of those prayer meetings was ever dull or boring. We did not raise our arms in the air, or strum guitars, or bang tambourines. But the thanks offered up to God were from the heart. I have found ever since those days that if ever a prayer meeting seems bogged down the finest tonic is to have a time of prayer and thanksgiving.

At the end of the summer term in 1956 I left school, and not having to do National Service because of bad eyesight, worked first in the hop fields of Kent and then on a chicken farm in Surrey. Bishop Faulkner Allison of Chelmsford had nominated me for the Church of England selectors. He insisted that before going to theological college I should work in London's East End at Canning Town. There I enjoyed four months working under the Rev David E. Gardiner at the Dockland Settlement No. 1. The work was in youth clubs for twelve to fourteen year old boys. I think this was one of the happiest times of my life. And it was then that I came into the next experience of prayer.

At about that time Revival Prayer Fellowships were springing up and nights of prayer were being held across the country on the first Friday of each month. We were no exception. As far as I recall we started by drinking coffee in the kitchen after we had closed the clubs and cleared away equipment. Then at eleven pm into the Settlement Chapel we went for the first session. We prayed through until six am with coffee breaks at two am and four am. David Gardiner insisted we all went to bed at six am for at least two hours so that we could cope adequately with the next day's work. There were other breaks, too, so that people could give reports of their work and mention prayer requests. It was all very relaxed. One brother always went to sleep kneeling down. Nobody minded. He didn't snore and we woke him up at the next coffee break.

This pattern I have maintained at Pip'n'Jay. We do not have regular nights of prayer, but when we do, we tend to start at eleven pm and go through to six the next morning. We usually divide the time into half-hour periods of prayer with five-minute breaks for fellowship and at least two twenty-minute intervals for coffee. Such periods of prayer have a lot going for them. The people who come mean business and there is a tremendous sense of anticipation afterwards – what is God going to do this time? And you are never disappointed. God honours such times. Look at what happened in the 1960s. I believe it was directly as a result of those monthly revival prayer meetings that the Charismatic renewal swept through England.

In 1965 when Pip'n'Jay was given a three-year trial period to see if it was viable as a church, we called a night of prayer. Matthew 6.33 outlines the programme God gave us. Putting his Kingdom first meant giving money away to mission outside our own parish. Well, we're still there, and still open for business. Although our own finances have been difficult at times, we have had all we need to function effectively and thousands of pounds have been given away. God willing, by the end of 1984 we shall have given half a million pounds to missions since 1965. God does answer prayer. Expectancy makes corporate prayer come alive.

Personal Prayer Problems

In the autumn of 1957 I began training for the ministry at Tyndale Hall Theological College, Bristol. After making a very obvious discovery that I was not an academic type it became a bit of an endurance test. But erudite studies aside there were practical lessons to be learned. If Friday mornings were to be suffered on account of the inevitable all-College choir practice, Tuesday after lunch prayer meetings were an oasis in the desert. At these short half-hour sessions we prayed for missionaries. There was a variety of groups to choose from. I settled for the Arctic prayer group and as a result have had an interest in that area ever since. It was all very simple and rather like a half-hour session from a night of prayer. For this first five or so minutes someone gave a report, outlined prayer requests, and then we prayed for the next twenty or so minutes. It is a very simple formula, and one we still use at Pip'n'Jay, especially when we have a missionary convention. We call a prayer meeting and have three to four such sessions, each one devoted to a different area of the world.

At Tyndale Hall we also had nights of prayer for revival. Not many students attended, and they are certainly not to be reprimanded. We were after all at College to get academic qualifications, and they were handing out no certificates for proficiency in prayer. But the interesting thing is that after all these years, old college friends with whom I still fellowship are nearly all those who prayed the night away.

As a good evangelical I had been well instructed in the importance of having one's 'QT'. Quite Times morning and evening were almost an essential to salvation. Evenings were relatively easy. I am a night person. I can appreciate mornings as much as anyone else. I thank God for the freshness of the air, the hoar frost on the grass, the bird song and all the rest of it, just so long as I can thank him in bed. I can get up reasonably early, sometimes very early, but it really is a waste of time. I stare stupidly at the ceiling, drink coffee, and generally do not rejoin the human race until elevenses. At college we had to go through the service of Morning Prayer every day plus the Litany once a week. Morning Prayer was held at seven-fifteen. Friends tell me that on the rare occasions I did attend, I was very correct, and stood, knelt, sat, responded, sang, said 'Amen', or whatever else the liturgy demanded of me. I was, they say, a very good Anglican. The trouble was that on returning to my room after Chapel I had no recollection at all of what had been going on, except that I had actually made it to Chapel for once. Anyway, down on my knees for the old QT and after five minutes I was sound asleep.

One of my spiritual heroes is John Wesley. I had managed to get hold of an eight-volume copy of his journal. He never wasted any time, it would seem, and was always looking for new ways to use his time more profitably. He decided he was sleeping too much, so he began to rise an hour earlier. The hour saved was spent in prayer. He felt very much better physically and spiritually, so he cut his sleep by another hour. Well, if it was good enough for Wesley it was good enough for Widdecombe. A system that lasted Wesley the remainder of his life benefited me for all of two days. It is one thing to daydream or doze in an afternoon lecture, but crashing out completely is quite another.

I came across an article by Oswald J. Smith, Pastor Emeritus of the People's Church, Toronto, whose writings had already influenced my life and set down patterns for my future ministry. I think the article was in the form of a little tract which dealt with the three hindrances to prayer. I believe in some degree or another every Christian experiences these very common problems. First there are interruptions – by family, friends, telephone and door bell. People who have not contacted you for years always call when you have at last found a moment to pray. Secondly, wandering thoughts afflict you as never before when you're trying to communicate with God. One moment I am praying for my missionary in India, and the next thinking about the next cross country race and imagine myself taking the lead halfway down Ladies Mile on Clifton Down. Thirdly, there is drowsiness. The best cure in the world for insomnia is to pray.

Oswald Smith's solutions were simple and practical. He

said steps must be taken to get away from interruptions. Over the years I have tried to do this. I have tried to find a room where there are no phones and I can lock the door. Taking a walk outside has been one answer. Entering a quiet church building has been another. Establishing a regular time so that the family know and try not to disturb me is another solution. This latter was a complete disaster in my case, not because the family refused to co-operate, but because of my inability to find the right and regular time.

Second, the problem of wandering thoughts is a problem of our own making. Somehow or another we accept that the correct method of communicating with Almighty God is silent prayer. I know the Bible tells us to be still and know that he is God. Of course, there is a place for silent prayer and meditation (providing one meditates positively on the word of God). But in fact in the Bible the norm for prayer is to pray aloud. I can think of two places where people prayed silently. The Pharisee prayed with himself. His prayer was so smug and self-satisfied, he dare not pray aloud! The other was Hannah. She prayed silently, only her lips moved. It was so unusual that old Eli thought she was drunk. Speaking aloud to God has been one of the most helpful aids to my prayer life that I can think of. Speaking aloud makes concentration natural and easy. If breaking the sound barrier in the prayer meeting is your problem, try breaking it in your own personal prayer time first.

Thirdly, Oswald Smith's answer to drowsiness was to walk. You may walk in your sleep but it is highly unlikely that you will sleep in your walk. Bowing one's head and closing one's eyes is an open invitation for sleep to overtake you. Call a meeting of Christians to prayer and watch the transformation. For the most part you have a wide awake audience, bright-eyed, and intelligent. 'Let us pray,' you say. Faces go blank, eyes close and bodies sag in their seats. You might as well have said, 'Let us nod off.' Of course there isn't always room to walk about in a large prayer group. But at Pip'n'Jay we make it clear that it is not necessary to close one's eyes. After all, how can you watch and pray if you shut your eyes? We encourage folk to sit up and look up. Those who actually pray aloud are asked to stand when they do so. We often have the whole meeting standing for a while. If it is a night of prayer or a daylong session, we organise the chairs so that there is room for people to walk if they wish. The best times of corporate prayer I have ever had have been in one of the larger rooms at the church with just two or three others. Chairs are cleared away and we walk and talk to God, achieving nearly maximum concentration and total wakefulness.

Dr J. Edwin Orr visited college and I was volunteered to look after him. I knew that this senior Christian, experienced in the history of revivals, was a personal friend of Dr Oswald Smith. As I shared with him how helpful Oswald Smith's advice had been to me, especially about walking, Dr Orr laughed. He told me, 'Oswald Smith prays a lot in his study. He walks up and down praying. But he always has his eyes shut. He's bumped into no furniture yet. It's a daily miracle.'

Fixing a Date
All these lessons were precious and have stayed with me through my ministry. I was ordained in 1962 and almost immediately began work with a group of young people, some of whom are still with me today. Prayer has always been a vital part of our church life. In June 1967 I had every reason to be content. I had just been appointed Priest-in-Charge of Pip'n'Jay. The fellowship was well launched as a centre for evangelism and mission. Finances were improving and attendances were going up. Yet spiritually I felt like a squeezed-out dish cloth. My own personal prayer life was almost non-existent. Ten minutes' interview with God each day and I am sure his was the greater relief when the session was over. I knew things should not be like that. I knew that I personally needed renewal. And renewal came through our involvement with what is called the Charismatic Movement. I reached a point where I asked God to baptise me with the Holy Spirit. I did not feel any different. I did not at that

24

time speak with tongues, that was an experience to follow later. But I had the renewal I had sought. I actually wanted to spend time with God. The problem had changed. Before it was a question of how to fill ten minutes. Now it was where to find enough time. God and I were friends again, and friends like to talk.

The spiritual gift called tongues upsets some believers. If that's you, please skip this paragraph. If I believe in the validity of prayer I also believe in the validity of tongues. First and foremost, tongues is a prayer language. It is not the best gift for public meetings, if it needs interpretation, because this takes time. This is why the apostle Paul allowed only three messages in tongues in any one meeting (1 Corinthians 14.27).

The gift comes into its own on the personal level. Paul calls it 'praying with the spirit'. I have found it helpful in three ways: tongues helps me to pray practically; the gift helps me to worship God; it also aids my participation in the public prayer meeting. In Romans 8.26 Paul tells us that when we get stuck in our own prayers, the Holy Spirit will help us out. I can pray reasonably intelligently for that missionary friend of mine serving God in the Diocese of the Arctic, because I have his prayer letter in front of me. But that letter is now three months out of date. I want to pray for his needs today. I haven't a clue what they are, but the Holy Spirit knows my friend's situation precisely. So having prayed as best I know in my natural language, I pray on in my super-natural language allowing God by his Spirit to pray through me. This makes tongues a very practical gift. In the same way when I want to worship and praise God and I run out of words, there is another language to use to lift my soul and give God the glory. In the public prayer meeting I personally am encouraged when people 'back' whoever is praying aloud. One can say an 'Amen', or a 'Yes, Lord'. One can also quietly pray in tongues. I find this most supportive when I am praying. Actively supporting others who are praying is also another way of helping concentration and staying awake. But Paul's words about doing things decently and in order need to be heeded. The 'backing' should never become so loud that the person praying can no longer be heard.

As you have gathered, I am not the most disciplined person in the world. My latest problem has been finding the time to pray. Renewal means I enjoy prayer but it does not make me immune from the negative thoughts imparted by Satan: 'Do I really need to go to the prayer meeting tonight? God knows how tired I am, he'll understand if I stay home and have an early night.' (He probably will, but he won't understand why the telly stayed on so late!) I know only one way of dealing with negative waves – take positive action. Get up and go to the prayer meeting. I find that when I attend a prayer meeting reluctantly I always come away glad that I made the effort to go.

But what about finding time for personal prayer? Pip'n'Jay is a fairly active church. The programme is quite hectic. In recent years I have been the Rural Dean which has meant an extra load of administration. Although I have enjoyed it in a masochistic sort of way, I'm very thankful that my term in that particular office will soon be over. Opportunities also occur to travel and minister abroad and numerous invitations come in to visit other churches at home. Endless activity is no substitute for prayer. And I am well aware that work done in God's name without God's power is next to useless. So how to find the time is the very real problem.

Another spiritual hero of mine is Oral Roberts. From time to time he spends a whole day in the prayer tower at the university that bears his name. He does this so that he can pray for his own prayer partners. At Christmas two or so years ago I was opening the mail. I watched the growing pile of prayer letters and I wondered how on earth I was ever going to find time to read them let alone pray over the contents. It dawned on me that in many other homes people were opening my own prayer letter and thinking exactly the same. I decided to have a prayer day. I booked it in my diary at least a month ahead. On the day appointed I locked myself in the church. People often ask what on earth I've got to pray about all day. Reading all the prayer letters and praying for the writers can take the morning completely. Going through the church membership roll and praying for each name however briefly in both English and in tongues, takes most of the afternoon. And I've not mentioned time to mention personal needs, family, my diary etc. A day can be filled with no difficulty at all.

It is not only pastors and preachers who can benefit from such a day. Below there follows a programme I have suggested for anyone in our church who wants to try it. It was designed for someone doing it for the first time, and also someone who had decided to spend the day fasting.

A Prayer Day Time Table

9.30 am   Sit at a table, write on a piece of paper all the things that currently concern you. Then pray about them. Pray out loud. This is a sort of clearing of the decks for action. Use whatever position you like for prayers. Experiment! Try flat on your face, and walking up and down the room.

10.30 am   Sing a chorus. (If you can't sing, don't worry. God doesn't mind. He just loves to hear his children praise him.) Get in your favourite armchair and read your Bible. From now and until 4 pm read roughly half an hour from the Old Testament and then half an hour from the New. In the Old Testament, start at Jonah, in the New, start at Mark's Gospel. Any time during the course of the day that you feel God is prompting you to praise or pray, stop reading and do it. Then start reading again. Observe roughly the suggested breaks.

11 am   Make a cuppa!

1 pm   Another cuppa and ten minutes walk outside, even if it's raining.

2.45 pm   Cuppa!

4 pm   Finish. You're surprised how quickly the time
          has gone. Get your diary and fix your next date
          with God.

Like every other Christian God hasn't finished with me yet.
I'm sure there are many more exciting things to learn about
prayer. I pray this chapter and indeed this whole book will
help you. But there is one thing I am completely convinced
about. You can read this book and a hundred others on the
subject of prayer. All I am sure will be helpful, some will
even be interesting, and others challenging. But the only
way you will ever learn to pray is by actually doing it.

Bob Gordon

Prayer: The Heart of the Matter

Bob Gordon is an ordained minister of the United Reformed Church. Born in Dumfriesshire, Scotland, he studied under Professor F. F. Bruce at Manchester University before becoming minister and chaplain in the University of Durham for eight years.

Until recently he was Lecturer in Old Testament at London Bible College. He now exercises a widespread preaching ministry at home and overseas.

He is Director of Roffey Christian Training Centre which is part of the ministry of the Bethany Fellowship in Sussex. He is the author of *How Much More?* which was published by Marshalls in 1983, and *Out Of The Melting Pot*, published by Marshalls in 1984.

I discovered a new depth in prayer about ten years ago. It was at a conference for clergy run by the Fountain Trust. Someone had been speaking from the sixth chapter of Isaiah when a profound thing happened to me. It was as though God himself walked out of the text into my experience.

What I discovered then is that at the heart of real prayer is a deep encounter with God. I came to understand that prayer is not so much words as the movement of God in the soul. It is communion between man's spirit and the Spirit of God. The cost of that is profound for with that experience came the deepest awareness of sin and darkness that I have ever known. I knew exactly what Isaiah meant when he said that he was lost and that he was a man of unclean lips. At the time of the encounter I was sitting in a low chair with wooden arms. So real was the awareness of God and the overwhelming sense of darkness and unworthiness that went with it that I could not move. It was as though I was being pushed through the bottom of the chair by the weight of the feeling and I recall vividly feeling utterly overcome with a sense of hopelessness and futility.

In that moment I came to realise the cost of true prayer. The first movement in prayer, from the human point of view, must be exposure of the soul. To know that bareness and to recognise honestly one's true position before a holy God is to be taken to a depth of self-realisation that is unacceptable to the flesh. Most of us recoil at the thought of an encounter such as that. Perhaps that is why to this day I have a certain reluctance in my flesh about being really open in the exercise of prayer, because if I am to know God in prayer it will mean first that he will know me.

I must have sat in that chair for some twenty minutes. Everybody else had left the room and had gone downstairs for supper. Then two friends noticed my absence and returned. They didn't hold a conversation with me because it was evident to them that something deep had happened. One of them, Michael Harper, simply came and laid hands on my head and led in prayer. I don't recall what happened except that I had the strangest sensation. I felt as though I had had a near miss in a car accident or something like that. I felt myself trembling and light inside. I went to bed like that but woke up next morning to the sun streaming in the room and the discovery that the sun of righteousness had risen with healing in his wings in my inner being. Somewhere in the old book of Ecclesiasticus is the saying, 'As is his majesty so too is his mercy.'

That was the second element in that experience of prayer. The overwhelming experience of the holiness of God was coupled with an equally deep knowledge of the mercy of God. Those two principles have governed my understanding of prayer ever since. On the one hand, we draw near to One who is far greater and holier than ourselves. Like Moses, we are bidden to take our shoes off our feet for the ground on which we stand is holy ground. On the other hand, we come to one who, as the Psalmist recalls, does not deal with us according to our sins. The sense of the greatness of God and the reality of the goodness of God that I found back there have governed every approach I have made in prayer whether in my personal experience or in ministry into the life of another person.

I made a second deep discovery in prayer about five years ago. It was at a time when my wife and I were facing important challenges with regard to our lives and ministry. It had become clear to us that we should leave the pastorate of our church in Durham and make ourselves available to work in a wider sphere, sharing and teaching what God is doing today in the power of the Holy Spirit. The difficulty was that there was no obvious way in which this was to happen save through the strong conviction on the part of many friends that it was right for us to do this. We went to London to meet some leading figures in the renewal movement and to discuss with my own denominational leaders the implications of such a move. During that time we stayed with some Christian friends in Wimbledon.

We spent two very frustrating days speaking with a number of people in our own United Reformed Church and elsewhere but it seemed that through it all there was no word from the Lord. At the end of the second day we returned exhausted and dispirited to the house where we were staying. To my amazement and discomfort we walked into the beginning of a charismatic house prayer meeting. We stole quietly into the back of the room and sat discreetly in the depths of a large settee. The meeting proceeded with the usual mixture of praise and prayer until suddenly, towards the end, a woman started to speak at the other side of the room. She said that the Lord had given her a very strong picture in her mind which, she believed, was for someone there in a particular way.

The picture was in two parts. The first was of herself standing on the veranda of a large country house, looking out over the gardens, which were very smart, neatly laid out with paths and little hedges. Her gaze moved down the garden until at the far end she saw a copse of trees. In the trees she saw a building. But when she looked more closely she noticed that the building was really a folly, built only for decoration. The next part was of the same woman standing this time, not in the orderly scene of the country house, but in the middle of a dense wood. The branches of the trees were all entangled and the undergrowth was very thick. She was standing in a clearing but there was no obvious path out of the clearing in any direction. However, she felt thoroughly happy and secure because the rays of bright sunlight were shining directly into the clearing and bathing her with warmth.

When she had finished describing the picture in its two parts she went on to say that she felt that this was appropriate to someone present and that God was telling them not to follow the path that seemed to be so well laid out because the end of this was only folly. They were to stand in the sunlight of God's presence even though at the moment there seemed to be no way out of the clearing. God would show the way and they were to trust him.

The effect of that picture and its interpretation was almost as profound for me as the experience five years before at the clergy conference. It was as though a bolt from the blue had hit me. I looked at my wife and we knew right away that this was the reason we had come to London. God had spoken to us but in a way that we had not expected and with a word that we had not looked for. The essence of that word has become for me the hallmark of my life for God. I know that what God has called me to is a life of trusting him. I find that very hard because my natural inclination is not to trust anyone but I look back over the five years that have gone and that word has been fulfilled in an outstanding way. There have been many times since then when I have stood in a clearing waiting for God to show the way but never have I been able to doubt that this is his purpose.

This second experience of prayer taught me two important lessons at least. First, that through prayer it is God's intention to bring a word of direction into what would otherwise be a pretty meaningless experience. When I think back to this experience I always recall the words of Isaiah the prophet: 'Your ears will hear a voice behind you, saying, "This is the way; walk in it"' (Isaiah 30.21).

That experience of hearing God speaking directly gave us no new information about what was going to happen. But it created faith. When God speaks to us that is what happens. It transforms the situation from one of emptiness and hopelessness to one in which there is the reality of faith.

The second lesson it taught me was that real prayer operates in and through the gifts of the Holy Spirit. I have come to believe that almost everything in prayer has to do with God rather than man. We need to take time and make our hearts available but it is God who takes the great initiatives in prayer. God moves by his Spirit and creates conviction. God moves by his Spirit and brings those special gifts to light in our lives through which he acts in the power of prayer. The gifts of the Holy Spirit are given to enable and enrich our life in prayer. Paul rightly points out in Romans 8 how weak we are in prayer without the help of the Holy Spirit: 'In the same way, the Spirit helps us in our weakness. We do not know what to pray (NIV margin: how to pray), but the Spirit intercedes for us with groans that words cannot express' (Romans 8.26).

But God's greatest challenge to me had still to come. It had to do with faith. Jesus said: 'You may ask me for anything in my name, and I will do it' (John 14.14). The question was, is that true?

I have come to see that the real heart of prayer is faith. The words of Hebrews 11.6 have always struck me forcibly, especially as they appear in the older Authorised Version: 'He that cometh to God must believe that he is, and that he is a rewarder of them that diligently seek him.'

A year or so ago that challenge came home to me in a powerful way. For the last few years I have lived with a vision. This was the vision of a place where men and women could come for a period of time to be taught and to share in the things of God in the power of the Holy Spirit, a place where they could approach the Scriptures in a spiritual and systematic way and where they could learn and experience at first-hand the power of the Holy Spirit in ministry.

Out of the blue one day a brochure was handed to me. It was a glossy estate agent's brochure advertising a college about four miles away that had come up for sale. This place had been the national training headquarters of the RSPCA. It was a purpose built teaching unit, fitted out to the last detail. One glance at the description told me that it was tailor-made for the dream that had been there all that time. I turned the brochure over and looked at the asking price. Over £600,000!

I slipped the brochure in my desk drawer and quietly

forgot it but over the next three weeks it seemed that every time I opened the drawer the brochure popped up. Finally I gave it to Colin Urquhart, my colleague in the word. His response was the same. We put it away. However, a few weeks later our solicitor telephoned to say that the following Friday final bids were being accepted for the college which would then be sold. I felt the old urgency coming back to my spirit and called on Colin. We agreed to meet for prayer.

A couple of days later we prayed together. During that time God made clear through the witness of the Spirit that we should offer £570,000 for the property, plus £10,000 for the fixtures and fittings. The next morning, which was Friday, we submitted our offer through our solicitor. At midday the phone rang and we were told that against all the odds our offer had been accepted. It was not that there was no opposition – at least three other worthwhile tenders had been received – but our extra £10,000 had made all the difference. Here was the principle of revelation through prayer at work once again.

That was only the beginning, because at that moment we did not have a penny. We needed £57,000 within four weeks to provide the deposit, followed by the remainder within a couple of months. The way the deposit came was a miracle in itself. On the day it was due I could account for the whole amount less £4,500. Two things were required, I felt, before we could place the deposit and so enter into a binding contract. One was the rest of the money; the other was some witness from outside the Fellowship of which I am part to the rightness of going ahead with the deal. We had only an hour or so to go to the final time for the deposit. So we prayed.

Some very interesting things happened. Firstly, with about half an hour to go, a letter was delivered to me. It had arrived earlier but had failed to reach me. It was a promise in writing from someone well outside the Fellowship of a gift of £4,500. But the striking thing about the letter was the fact that the writer intimated that whilst he could not yet forward the gift he felt he had to write to say that he felt that this was in some way connected with a deposit for some property we were engaged in buying. Little did he know just how important his statement was!

Then a few moments later a gift arrived for about £3,500. Then the telephone rang. It was a woman in the Fellowship who had been helping another Christian lady to clear out some old rubbish from her house. They had been clearing boxes and other oddments from under the stairs when suddenly they discovered an old shoe box with £995 in it in old pound notes. They found that these could still be accepted as tender and had just rung up to say that they thought the money should go towards the purchase of the college. The words of Jesus were running true to promise.

Over the next four months God provided over £300,000 towards the project. But we were still £300,000 short when it came to only four days before the last possible date for completion. The intervening months had been a real test of faith and during that time the power of prayer became very special to me. In that period we had met together many times to claim the promises of faith. I was absolutely sure that God was going to honour his promises and make provision so that the college could be bought. But how?

The phone rang on the Monday night of that final week. It was Colin Urquhart, back from a ministry trip to Australia. He had returned via Singapore where he had stopped off for twenty-four hours. He asked if I had all the money yet. I said we hadn't but that I was sure God was going to provide it in time. He then said quietly that he had it.

What had happened was very simple. He had been on the way to the plane in Singapore with a Christian friend. That friend had asked him how things were and when Colin told him about the college he asked if we had all the money yet. When he heard that we needed to find some of the money he simply wrote a cheque for £50,000 and arranged for the other £250,000 to be telexed to England by the following Friday morning.

Today I live and work as Director of Roffey Place Christian Training Centre. It exists to bring the same lessons of faith into the lives of the men and women who come here to study. I believe that the challenge of faith in prayer is the greatest challenge that faces the Church in our country today. It is this which really shows whether or not we are willing to allow God to be God or not.

All this means that, for me, prayer has become very important. It stands at the centre of my life and ministry. But what is so vital to me is not so much the words that are used as the attitude of heart: there is awe and wonder, listening and hearing, faith and obedience.

When we pray we are putting faith into action. Among the many things that could be said three are of particular importance to me.

First, when we pray we grow. Prayer has changed my ideas of holiness. I grew up with a very legalistic notion of holiness, based chiefly on the words 'Thou shalt not'. Now I see things differently. Through waiting on God in prayer we come to know God. And the more we know God the more we know ourselves. No wonder it is said that the greatest saints are conscious most of sin within. The more a man is conscious of God, the more he is conscious of his own weakness and lack of holiness. This sense of the holiness of God causes us to grow because it creates a thirst to be like God and as we continue to live in his presence in prayer we begin to reflect his character in our human nature. Surely that is what Paul meant when he wrote: 'We, who with unveiled faces all reflect the Lord's glory, are being transformed into his likeness with ever-increasing glory' (2 Corinthians 3.18).

The refining power of the holiness of God and the creative power of his goodness lie at the heart of holiness. Holiness is no longer learned by rote but in relationship. 'Be holy, for I am holy' is the winsome appeal of God who makes himself known in the heart through prayer by the Holy Spirit.

The second area is ministry. Prayer is the means by which

we can release the power of faith into the lives of other men and women. I remember very well the first time that I became conscious of this.

I had been involved in counselling a university student who had been experiencing dreadful nightmares and who, for some unknown reason, was regularly waking up through the night in terror. Every agency, medical and otherwise, had tried to help, to no avail. He was sent to me last of all, for a bit of religion. I saw him for three weeks in a row, to no good purpose. On the last occasion he was about to leave when I was prompted by the Spirit to ask him where he had spent his previous holiday. It transpired that he had been on holiday with a friend at the home of a woman who had been a witch. Since that time he had been having these terrible nocturnal experiences. I asked if he minded if I prayed. I had just started praying and mentioned the name of Jesus when I heard a sound. Looking up, I saw that he had fallen at my feet, out cold. I panicked inwardly but kept praying and found myself praying in the experience of the resurrection. It was as though I was actually standing in the empty tomb. There was another noise – I looked, and there was the student standing directly in front of me, looking into my eyes. To my knowledge that was the last time he ever had a nightmare. Through the power of prayer the bondage of Satan had been broken, even though the prayer had been far from extraordinary and the knowledge of the counsellor about such things very scant.

That was a tremendous lesson about the power that is available through prayer in the name of Jesus to enable us to minister into the lives and needs of men and women today.

The third area is spiritual warfare. 'Pray in the Spirit on all occasions', says Paul in Ephesians 6, at the end of his discourse on spiritual warfare. Through prayer, the power of the Kingdom of God is addressed against the power of the kingdom of darkness.

One writer put it well for me when he said: 'Prayer is insisting upon Jesus' victory and the retreat of the enemy on each particular spot. The enemy yields only what he must.

He yields only what is taken. Therefore ground must be taken step by step. Prayer must be definite.'

Often the Holy Spirit will enable us to pray in the power of tongues because what is being resisted or opposed is far beyond the expression of our normal language. God takes hold of our faculties and gives us the language of heaven to oppose and tear down the powers of darkness. Frequently as we pray we find we are led by the Holy Spirit into the realm of spiritual warfare far beyond the bounds of our own experience. Here the essence of intercessory prayer lies in making our beings available to God so that he can work in and through them and write his agenda on our hearts and minds. That is why, in this kind of praying, groups will sometimes find themselves involved in praying for subjects far beyond the limits of their own sphere or experience.

In the end I could say, I suppose, that for me prayer is not so much a programme, more a way of life.

Heather Wraight

Why Pray When You Can Panic?

Heather was born into a Christian home in the late 1940s. From an early age she knew God wanted her to be a missionary. After school she trained as a nurse and midwife, specialising in the care of premature babies.

She studied at Redcliffe Missionary Training College before joining WEC International to work with Radio Worldwide. After ten years in programme production she was elected Director in 1983.

The green light flashed, and Ivan Mark announced, 'Dhup Aur Chaya, programme number 158 starts in five seconds from now.' Up came the music, and we were off. Ivan and his wife Thelma chatted in Hindi, their own language, for a minute or two, and then the script called for an item that had already been recorded. I pressed the button to start the tape, but it was the wrong recording, and we heard some Indian music instead. We started again – 'Dhup Aur Chaya, programme number . . .' This was a fairly complicated programme technically, but one I had done many times before, 157 times in fact. That afternoon there were two major differences. It was the start of a new series, with several changes which we hoped would make it more attractive to listeners. Also we had another person in the studio to ask questions during the programme. That helper was not a Christian, although she was happy to be involved. Her visit to our studio relieved the monotony of being an Asian wife, confined to her home in south London.

We reached exactly the same point in the programme – and ground to a halt again, for a different reason. What was wrong with me? I sat and looked at the script and the machines in front of me. But the more I looked, the more confused I became. 'Don't panic!' I told myself. 'Just relax and think straight – now what do you do first to sort out this muddle?' But no! I could not work it out. At one time we had a notice above the window between the control room and studio saying simply 'Psalm 12 v 1'. That verse starts 'Help, Lord'. I needed that help now – but my mind kept worrying away at the problem I had created for myself.

Then it dawned on me. The problem really was not a technical one, it was a spiritual one.

We often take far too much for granted spiritually. Sure, we had prayed in a general way about the day's programmes, we always do. But this was special – a new series, a non-Christian helper – and Satan was interfering. I sat back in my chair and claimed the authority of the name of Jesus over Satan's attack. I asked the Lord to remove the confusion from my mind, because the Bible tells us he is not a God of confusion or disorder, but of peace. As I prayed, my thinking cleared. I re-read the script, and saw immediately how it should be handled. Ivan, Thelma and I all silently breathed, 'Thank you, Lord', as this time the programme flowed through smoothly.

It was a salutary reminder to us all. It is easy for prayer to become a habit. But just because we always pray before we start a recording session, it can turn into simply another part of the routine – get machines, tape and so on ready; put microphones in place; check scripts; pray ... quite mechanical. We forget that we are in a spiritual battle.

A. W. Tozer reminds us that 'In an effort to get the work of the Lord done we often lose contact with the Lord of the work.' How many times have you been to a committee meeting which started with prayer, but within a few minutes became quite indistinguishable from a secular business meeting? We invite the Lord to help us, and then ignore him completely. Yet we should be different, after all, it is not the mouthing of a prayer that shows we are Christians. Many organisations which are quite secular begin their gatherings with prayer. Our trouble is that we often don't let God answer!

Then there are the occasions like that recording session when we forget we are in a spiritual battle. The more effective we are as Christians, the less Satan likes it, and the harder he will try to disrupt our activities. Yet we should be able to recognise our enemy and know how to deal with him, because Jesus has given us his authority.

It was Alfred, Lord Tennyson who said, 'Greater things

are wrought by prayer than this world dreams of', and Jesus himself said, 'Anyone who has faith in me will do what I have been doing. He will do even greater things than these, because I am going to the Father.' Many of us have puzzled over that verse in John 14. How can we possibly do 'greater things' than Jesus did? I believe one of the ways is through prayer. Satan was defeated by the death and resurrection of Christ, and so we can and should know victory over him.

Nowadays we are much more aware of what is going on around the world than Jesus as a man could ever have been. During his earthly life, he was limited to touching the lives of those with whom he had personal contact, either directly or second-hand like the Centurion's servant. Now, in prayer, we can touch lives we have never met, people who are miles away from us.

Our communications today are amazing. When my grandfather was a child there was no radio, and certainly no television. Transport was on foot or possibly by horse, and for most people their world was the area within walking distance of home. Now, only a few decades later, the world is truly our parish. We hear of events at the other side of our globe within minutes of them happening, and with the advent of cable television and direct broadcast satellites, where will the information explosion end? Yet how do we as Christians use all this knowledge? Surely it gives us the opportunity to pray that the Lord will give his victory in situations we cannot reach in any other way.

At Radio Worldwide we regularly set aside a whole day for prayer. Soon after one of these days a friend called. 'You were praying for me on Thursday', was his greeting. He went on to explain that he had been tackling a particularly knotty problem at work, when suddenly, at about three in the afternoon, he felt flooded with warmth and joy and a sense of the Lord's presence. He immediately felt that we had been praying for him. I thought back through the items we had prayed for on the Thursday. Yes! About three o'clock we were praying for Derek and others like him who help us in their spare time.

At church we had news that one of our missionaries was going through a particularly bad time. She was ill, with no access to treatment, depressed and lonely. Satan seemed to be throwing everything he could at her. The situation was shared in a prayer meeting. Half a dozen of us gathered round to pray specifically for her. We realised that a prayer such as 'Lord bless our sister and help her to cope' was woefully inadequate. We needed to battle spiritually on her behalf. As we waited on the Lord, he showed us how to pray, what to ask for, how to stand against Satan's attack on her. We none of us knew the intimate details of her problems, but the Lord did, and he was able to reveal to us the most effective way to pray. Thousands of miles away he would answer those prayers, and bring his victory.

Our radio programmes are made in south London. But we don't broadcast them ourselves. They go by post all over the world to the twenty or so stations which air them for us. With some of the stations we don't even know when during the week our programme is transmitted. We certainly don't know in detail who our listeners are, yet we expect God to speak to them. That doesn't remove our responsibility to make the programmes as interesting and as technically good as we can. But having done that, like the seed that Paul planted and Apollos watered, it is God who makes it grow. How quickly we lose sight of that. Contracts with the radio stations mean that in every series we make we have to average one programme each week – including the times when we are away from the office because of deputation, holidays, conferences, or even illness. The pressure of keeping up with deadlines can mean that once the programme is written, recorded, edited, copied and posted we feel as though our job has ended. Far from it, it has only just begun.

In *Born for Battle* R. Arthur Mathews wrote: 'Haven't we discovered that the technical excellence we are developing is still relatively powerless to produce the right kind of results? I believe that stronger and quicker development in God's work is impossible apart from multiplying prayer helpers.' And it is just as true in the work and witness of the local church as it is for folk like me who are in what is often called full-time service.

By touching lives thousands of miles away, or allowing God to work in situations which have no human solution, we are at least going some way towards doing 'greater things' than Jesus did.

It is a tremendous privilege to be able to pray together as a team, as we at Radio Worldwide do every morning before starting the day's work. But that is no substitute for our own personal relationships with the Lord. Personally I am an owl, not a lark. I find it much easier to work on into the night than to rise in the morning. And with no children to wake me up, or husband to pack off to work, it is sometimes just too tempting to turn over when the alarm goes off in what seems like the middle of the night. But I have found that I must have time alone with the Lord before starting on the business of the day.

In recent years it seems to have gone out of fashion in some circles to talk about a daily 'Quiet Time'. Personally I couldn't cope without it. I don't always find it straightforward. My grasshopper mind can take my thoughts miles away as soon as I start praying and my time can be frittered away. But unless my day is centred on the Lord at the start, much valuable time later may be wasted. It isn't the end of the world if I miss my Quiet Time occasionally, but if one day stretches into two or three, or a week, I soon notice a change in my relationship with the Lord.

It often shows up first in my relationships with my colleagues. Living and working with the same people has a lot of advantages, especially with the cost of living in London being what it is. But it also has its pressures. And isn't it always the little things that upset us?

I am a fairly tidy person, and at the end of the day my desk is usually left with everything neatly in place. Others of my colleagues are quite happy to keep all sorts of bits and pieces in apparent confusion. When I want them to find something it is so easy to feel frustrated or annoyed as they shuffle through the piles of paper looking for the particular item. On the other hand, it is equally maddening for them to discover that I have tidied away something which they left out for a purpose. Such little things can soon escalate into big problems, unless we have learnt how to love and pray for one another. I can't love these people on my own – we didn't choose to live and work together. But God made the selection, and he knows it is possible for us to get on well with one another. However it doesn't just happen; it sometimes takes much prayer and effort.

It is a wonderful discovery that prayer isn't limited to big things. It is just as much an attitude of life. I pray about all sorts of details, some of which my friends think are far too insignificant to bother God about! But why not? He is my heavenly Father. There are many occasions when I would ask a husband for advice, if I had one. I could panic – and used to quite often – but I've learned to ask the Lord instead. Actually I find that many of my friends turn to the Lord for such things too, even though they are married. Husbands aren't always there, and even when they are, they're only human. They don't have all the answers, and they can be too busy, or overtired. But God always has time to listen. I don't pretend to understand how he can hear and answer me when thousands of others all over the world are praying at the same time. But I do know he can.

Let me give you an example of the kind of thing I've discovered. He cares about – my bank statement! Now I was quite good at maths at school, but somewhere something has got a bit lost I think! My bank statement hardly ever tallies with what my cheque book says it should be, even though I only write at the most about twenty cheques in a month. I can add up the figures all right, but I can get in the most incredible muddle working out what should be in which column. Yet time and again as I sit and stare uncomprehendingly at a lost – or gained! – £5.23 or some such ridiculous figure, the Lord shows me exactly where it is.

And then there are parking meters. He's very good at

those! We have a communal meal on weekdays, which the ladies take it in turns to cook. Fruit and vegetables are considerably cheaper at our local market, but a week's supply for ten or twelve people is very heavy to carry. Time and again the Lord guides me to a parking meter within easy reach of the market. One time, I remember, I wanted to buy a sack of potatoes, and as I turned the corner at the end of the market a car was pulling away from the very first meter – and there were twenty minutes left on it too! Thank you, Lord.

I don't assume that he will do things like that for me, but I do pray about them, as I drive towards the place. In fact, I do quite a lot of praying while I'm driving. I fairly often travel longish distances on my own, going to meetings and conferences and so on. I could be very lonely, but I chat to the Lord as though he were sitting in the passenger seat next to me. Often inspiration for programmes, ideas for sermons, or solutions to problems come as I talk them through with him. I find it easier to sort out my thinking if I can discuss it with someone. The Lord has blessed me with some good friends both inside and outside my work, but it isn't always possible to share everything. Anyway, as Director of Radio Worldwide, I find there are some things that have to remain confidential. I am so glad that I learned to discuss things with the Lord before I was given this responsible position.

It is unusual for a mission leader to be a single lady. Leadership can be lonely enough for a couple, but long ago the Lord taught me that there is a great difference between loneliness and aloneness. I was very lonely when I first moved away from home and I prayed about it, asking the Lord for all sorts of things – a husband, friends, new interests, the ability to cope. But it was so easy for those prayers to turn into self-pity. It is a short step from there to becoming what someone has termed the President of the Poor Me Society! Praying about my own loneliness made me introspective, and often started a vicious circle which could lead to depression and even anger at God for leaving me single. So did I stop praying? No! Instead I started praying for others. That turned me inside out and made me think not only about them, but also about what God could do for them. The more I used my imagination in prayer for other people, the more I forgot about myself.

I'm not talking about the 'Lord bless all the missionaries in Africa' sort of prayer. I remember one of the staff at my Bible College hearing someone pray like that. She asked, 'How do you expect the Lord to answer that? Which missionaries do you mean, in what part of Africa, and what particular blessing did you have in mind for them?'

If we are going to pray in more detail, how do we know what to pray? Jesus tells us, 'Whatever you ask for in prayer, believe that you have received it, and it will be yours' (Mark 11.24). It doesn't always work though, does it? How many times have you asked for something, really believing God would give it – and he hasn't?

At the beginning of 1983 I injured my back. It will take me some time to live it down, because it happened at a Keep Fit class! I tore some ligaments in the lower part of my spine, and for several weeks it was almost impossible to sit. I could stand up or lie flat on the floor, but sitting down was agony and driving out of the question. Some years before God had healed my spine of a slipped disc dating from my nursing days, and also cured a mild deformity of my shoulder and neck joints which went back to my birth. So this time, in my panic, I immediately assumed that of course God would want to heal this injury – after all for several years my back had been perfect as a result of his intervention. I asked for prayer from the team at Radio Worldwide, and my local church elders. I claimed healing; I believed he would do it, but nothing happened!

It just didn't occur to me that perhaps God had other plans in allowing the injury. It turned out that this was his way to make me spend more time with him. I couldn't dash around filling every moment because I couldn't dash anywhere! Over several weeks I had many precious evenings when I prayed and thought and read – and he spoke to me.

50

He didn't answer my prayer and heal my back because he had something better in mind for me. What I ought to have asked was for him to reveal his will. In this case his will was to show me the root cause of various tensions and insecurities I had battled with for years. The answers didn't come quickly, because God was dealing deeply with me. But the result was a different kind of prayer for healing – not healing of torn ligaments, but healing of torn emotions.

The outcome was a much more relaxed Heather, with far more to give to the new responsibilities of leadership. Indeed, it is unlikely that I would have been given those responsibilities had the Lord not dealt with my tensions and insecurities. The team knew me well enough to recognise that until I was sorted out I could not cope emotionally with the extra pressures.

The significant thing was that God revealed his will – and that is a far cry from tacking on to the end of a prayer the words, 'If it be thy will'. I am talking about knowing what God's will is before we start praying – although admittedly we sometimes have to pray to find out what that will is. Now I know this could lead us off into another whole subject, and I am supposed to be writing about prayer. But as one of the modern posters says, 'If you aim at nothing, you're sure to hit it.'

Sometimes God reveals his will quite dramatically. Perhaps it's a scripture that comes to life, or God speaks through the counsel of a Christian friend, maybe during a sermon, or in our own devotional time. Radio Worldwide is part of the interdenominational missionary society WEC International. In WEC, God has given us a particular 'prayer sequence' which we often use in seeking his will about big projects. It starts with discussing the situation as a group. There is no rush about this, so that everyone has an opportunity to contribute. Then the leader clarifies what seems to be coming through the discussion. Only once we agree on what we're to pray about do we actually start praying. You see, once we really know God's will in any situation, we can expect, and even demand that he work it out.

Dick Davies is our Chief Engineer. He and Flora were eagerly awaiting the arrival of their first child. But the baby was born three months early, only a couple of days past what used to be considered the earliest point at which a baby had any likelihood of survival. Andrew was tiny – only 980 grams in weight – less than a bag of sugar. Nursing staff asked Dick if he would like his little son to be baptised – and having nursed such premature babies myself, I knew that was a sure sign that there wasn't much hope of him pulling through. Dick replied that they would rather have someone anoint Andrew and pray for him. I was chosen, partly as the new leader of the team, and also because of my experience with and love for these tiny infants.

The visit was to take place on Monday afternoon. Over the weekend I asked the Lord to reveal his will about Andrew. Of course we all desperately wanted him to survive, but I felt I needed some specific word from God for this situation. On Monday we were as usual eating lunch together. We always have a short reading and prayer together at the end of the meal. That day part of the reading was from Exodus 2.9. We read in the Living Bible: 'Take this child home and nurse him for me.' Suddenly we all knew this was God's word to us about Andrew. It was God's will for Flora to bring him home and nurse him – he would survive.

At the hospital, as I prayed with Dick, Flora and two Christian nurses, we knew that this tiny scrap of humanity would be all right – not only because we wanted it, but because God had said so. That didn't mean everything was plain sailing – there were many times in the next few months when we had to remind God of his promise, and again claim his touch on this little life. But because we knew God's will, we weren't praying in the dark. We were able to mix praise with our prayers because we knew that God was already answering.

Our faith wasn't in faith – in our own belief that God was capable of helping Andrew. Our faith was in the revealed will of God. In a very real sense it wasn't our responsibility, it was his.

Do I believe in prayer? I certainly do! I wouldn't be here if God hadn't answered prayer when I was born. There would be no point carrying on with my ministry if I didn't believe that by prayer God can turn our listeners into people who not only hear the word but also believe. And it would be impossible to live a victorious Christian life if I couldn't draw on God's resources through prayer. My natural nature would frequently panic and then, possibly, pray. But the more I grow spiritually the more I know that isn't the way forward – why panic when you can pray?

Clifford Fryer was born at Northolt, Middlesex in 1939 and was educated at St Clement Danes Grammar School. One of the last National Servicemen, he served in the Royal Army Educational Corps from 1960 to 1962, spending most of the time in Malta.

On returning to Britain he resumed his career as an industrial chemist, but had set his sights on the teaching profession, hoping to specialise in music. He was converted to Christ in September 1962 through the ministry of Dr Martyn Lloyd-Jones. Almost immediately he felt God's call to the Christian ministry and entered Spurgeon's College in 1966. He has served in Baptist Churches in Merton Park, Streatham and Ilfracombe (where he is at present Pastor).

He retains a keen interest in the arts. He enjoys writing and music, playing the piano in Christian meetings and conducting 'crusade' choirs when opportunities arise.

He is married with three sons: Jonathan (ten), David (nine) and Jeremy (four). In moments of relaxation you might find him engaged with them in back-yard cricket or front-room snooker. He and Anne are also foster-parents with two daughters: Elaine (eleven) and Emily (ten).

Clifford Fryer

Prayer: Anyone, Anywhere, Any Time, Anything

In the Shadow of Mr Hyde

It was 1963. I had been a Christian for about a year. I had recently made friends with a young Bible College student. He was very kind and had a deep love for the Lord, but he had about him that other-worldly look: dare I say it – almost dreamy. One day we fell into conversation about prayer.

'Have you heard of Praying Hyde?' he asked.

'No!' I replied. The question made me feel a bit of an outsider. This feeling came upon me fairly frequently as a new Christian with no Sunday School or church background. I was unfamiliar with all the jargon and had failed to crack the enigmatic code language spoken by many Christians: QT, YPF, NYLC, BMS, RBMU, LCM, OMF, OM, MWE, DV, WEC, and so on – what did it all mean?

'What! Never heard of Praying Hyde?' He looked a little reproachful.

'No. I don't think so.'

'He prayed six hours a day!'

I was stumped for a reply. I could only manage about ten minutes, but I had enjoyed it. It was a new experience talking to a heavenly Father rather than a blank wall in a lonely room.

'Praying Hyde!' I thought. 'The Napoleon of Prayer!'

And so he was. But the more I imagined his mighty advances and conquests through intercession, the more I saw myself as the Drummer Boy of Prayer.

Then it happened again.

'Have you heard of Praying Hyde?' shouted the preacher.

'Yes I have. He prayed for six hours a day,' I said to myself, feeling quite in on things.

'He prayed for eight hours! . . . *Every day!*' he roared, punching the air to reinforce the last two words.

'Wow!' I thought. 'The Bradman of Prayer.' There was John Hyde returning from the field, 'pavilioned in splendour and girded with praise', after another marathon innings on his knees, having smashed the enemy attack to all points of the compass. And there was I: the myopic Number Eleven of Prayer squinting at the oncoming ball, driving the air through the covers, and hearing that fatal sound of falling timbers behind me.

It was to happen yet once more. I was reading one of those ultra-spiritual books on revival which have the habit of showing up just when things aren't going too well in the Church and we're all wondering what is wrong with us.

'Of course, we have all heard of Praying Hyde.'

'Indeed we have,' affirmed the reader with some smugness. 'He prayed for eight hours! . . . *Every day!*'

'Hyde spent ten hours a day in prayer. It was a blessing to be with him in the prayer room. Intercession and praise came forth from his lips as sweet music unto God.'

'Wow!' I thought. 'The Beethoven of Prayer.' I could almost hear those sacred symphonies of prayer ascending to regale the ears of the Almighty, while my fleeting penny-ballads passed unnoticed.

I confess to a touch of poetic licence, but the incidents described above are based firmly on fact. We have our quota of heroes, from pulpit to prayer cell, but we have not always raised them up for the purpose of encouragement. We have sometimes used great men and women of God as guilt-goads to spur us on to greater efforts, or to box each other's ears in sermons intended for spiritual advancement.

I went through a time when I believed that to admit to any prayer problems was to risk the tag of 'unspiritual'. I had somehow got the idea that prayer solved everything quickly and painlessly. 'If you want revival, then pray. If you want victory over temptation, then pray. Prayer is the inexorable barometer of our spiritual lives. Plenty of it means that we are doing all right, little of it means we are backsliding almost beyond redemption.' I met preachers who added fifty per cent to the numbers attending their meetings, but felt the need to add one hundred and fifty per cent to the time they spent in prayer. It wasn't just the preachers. Some of their flocks were good at bleating on about lack of prayer in the church but were always too busy praying at home to attend the prayer meeting.

Some of my friends over-reacted to this kind of attitude and went so far as to reject the necessity of a regular time with the Lord as legalism but I believe there will always be a place for good habits and that regular prayer must be one of them. I cannot say that I have never missed a day. In some periods of my life more appointments with God have been missed than kept. It may be that in the hustle of modern living people pray less than they used to. There are major contenders for our time. I have found that time I had set aside for prayer has been seduced by the hypnotic television screen, or raped by the brutally demanding telephone.

As a fallible human being I have at times fallen far short of God's great purposes for the life of prayer. In sharing openly about my own prayer life I trust that I will not be defrocked, or whatever they do to Baptist ministers who have not reached perfection. Along with the large majority of God's people I strongly affirm that I believe in prayer. I have a deep hunger for growth and for more depth in communion with God and I refuse to be put off by the shame of having failed too often to meet with him. What greater miracle or privilege could there be than to talk to God himself? It has been my joy to talk to the Lord about the most personal areas in my life as well as the great purposes of his Kingdom. I believe in prayer because anyone can pray anywhere, at any time, about anything.

I Need Others

While the greatest incentive to prayer is God himself, I don't believe I would be where I am today without my brothers and sisters in Christ. From praying with others I have learned to pray myself. When I have begun to flag in faith they have joined me in intercession and together we have pressed through and seen glorious answers from God. At those times when God has said 'No' or 'Wait' they have helped me to understand what is going on or simply to accept God's will when I cannot see the whys and wherefores.

It took me eighteen months to break through the shyness barrier and pray aloud in a prayer meeting. Often a prayer would form on my lips but I dared not utter it. I can't quite say why. Maybe I didn't think I could pray as well as the rest. Maybe it was simply that I had never done it before. My painful self-consciousness deceived me into thinking that at a prayer meeting you are talking to man rather than God. Subsequent experiences incline me to think that this might not be entirely the fault of the new Christian. Some people will pray you a sermon. I once suffered the embarrassment of a young deacon praying against me. He must have felt the need to knock down my pride. When I asked the Lord for more to be converted and come into our church, he asked the Lord to keep us humble and teach us to be content with what we have.

These things aside, I have always found it easier to pray when others are there in support. I used to feel guilty about this. Satan would tell me it was because I was an exhibition-ist and quote scriptures about going into my closet, shutting the door and praying to my Father in secret. He never reminded me of what can happen when God's people come together in prayer. I must confess that I still prefer prayer meetings to private prayer. I can concentrate better. It helps me to pray out loud, something which I find difficult when I am alone with God, without any visible companion. This may be because some adults taunted me for it when a child, assuring me that talking to yourself was the first sign of madness. I believe it is right to pray aloud and look forward to the time when God enables me to find liberty in it.

Some of my most treasured memories come from times spent with others in prayer. How the Spirit of God can move on such occasions! It seems only yesterday when I was caught up in such a movement while I was a student at Spurgeon's College. I had been through an arid time, and was almost overcome by certain intellectual difficulties concerning the Gospels and the Acts of the Apostles in particular. As an orthodox evangelical I had believed that some manifestations of the Spirit such as prophecy, miracles and healing happened in the Old and New Testaments but that God had allowed them to die out now that the canon of Scripture was complete. In the course of studying for the London BD I encountered the more liberal view which said bluntly that such things do not happen now and therefore never happened in Acts. I could see the consistency of this argument, and felt that mine was ducking the issue, or even 'cooking the books'. It did me good to face up to others' views instead of retreating into a ghetto with uncertain walls. It drove me to God. He solved the dilemma by blessing me with his Spirit and putting me into a realm I had known little of before.

Some of those prayer meetings went on until two or three in the morning. It wasn't planned that way. It just happened. Nobody noticed the time. At times the Lord's presence was so real that I felt I could reach out and touch him. At one meeting no one could speak for two or three hours. To do so would have been unholy. My private prayer times were transformed as a result of what God did at those wonderful meetings. It was at that time that I discovered the power of praise and its connection with effective prayer. Praise does not twist God's arm for an answer, for that is unnecessary, but it does enhance our appreciation of his might and majesty and so generate the faith which secures answers from heaven.

I have found that faith and love are built up when brothers pray together in unity. God hates it when his people indulge in bickering, but loves it when they come together to seek his face. I did not find the early years of the Christian ministry very easy. I was sustained in no small measure by a prayer-friendship with the Rev Garth Moody of Wimbledon. We were led to set aside every Thursday morning for prayer. Everything, especially the demands of pastoral work, said it couldn't be done, but God said it must. For the first two or three months we received a stream of 'emergencies'. We resisted them, quickly realising that anything but matters of life and death could be dealt with just as well in three or four hours' time. At that time we were both heavily involved in deliverance ministry and we needed those hours with God. Later on other ministers joined us. God spoke to us through tongues, prophecy and vision and even more frequently fed us from the Scriptures. It was not time lost to the pastorate either. Many sermons were forged in the fire of those mornings. Some of our flock were healed, delivered and transformed through persistent intercession.

Courage is also engendered by praying together. In the three churches where I have been in full-time ministry I have been involved in leading Evangelism Explosion programmes. Few, if any, have found it easy to go out and meet others eyeball to eyeball with the gospel. Prayer does not diminish the task of visiting a home, but through it God gives the strength to walk up the path, push the door bell and mention his name. Countless times those whom we brought before God in prayer received Christ that very night.

Prayer is spiritual warfare. No man ever defeated an army single-handed, and neither can our stay-at-home prayers. This is one of the main reasons why I need my fellow soldiers. I understand that hunting lions always prey on the animal that gets separated from the flock. There is a certain element in my nature which tells me to keep away from church if there is something not quite right, or if I am having a tough time spiritually. This has more than once given Satan just the opportunity he was looking for. I hope

I have now learned that those times when my personal life with God is a bit groggy are the very times when I most need fellowship with strong Christians. The birds-of-a-feather syndrome, the temptation to gravitate to other disgruntled, weak Christians, must be resisted at all costs. My eldest son has just started life-saving lessons. I have noticed that more time is spent in building up the strength of his swimming than in teaching life-saving techniques. Without that basic strength he and the person he is attempting to save will drown each other!

Praying together is an earnest business, but there are lighter moments which are there to be enjoyed. I have found it important not to lose my sense of humour, and to be tolerant and loving when someone makes a blunder. Disciplining of the wilfully disruptive is a must, but much harm can be done in harsh silencing of those who genuinely know no better. It is well to remember that we have all made mistakes, even in prayer. I once heard an eccentric true-blue lady pray, 'Lord, please give Jim Callaghan and this awful Labour government a punch up the bracket.' (Now we know why Mrs Thatcher won the 1979 election so easily.) I had not been in the ministry very long when two pentecostal twin brothers visited our little housegroup and thought it lacking in what they called 'manifestations'. They decided to give it a shot in the arm by grunting non-stop throughout the whole meeting. Being new to the job, and unused to leadership, I was not quite sure what to do. I had just hit upon the idea of starting up a chorus when my wife leaned over and whispered in my ear:

> 'If you go down in the woods today,
> You're sure of a big surprise.'

I was glad that all had their eyes shut, as I had to stuff my handkerchief into my mouth and bite on it as hard as I could.

Boy Doesn't Meet Girl

Young men with a call to the ministry do not spend all their time praying for greater personal holiness or for the conversion of the nation. At least, I didn't, and neither did most of the others I knew! I actually had the nerve to pray for a wife. God answered it brilliantly, although it took him eight years. During those years of waiting he taught me many lessons about discipleship and prayer. I found my heavenly Father to be gentle, loving and even humorous at times, but he was always firm and never deflected from what he knew was best for his impatient and demanding child.

In my pre-Christian days I didn't have much confidence with members of the opposite sex. Though at the time I saw this as nothing but torture, I now look back on it as a blessing, as it saved me from becoming enmeshed in the casual but emotionally dangerous relationships favoured by the permissive society. After my conversion I expected God to produce Miss Right straight from heaven, so saving me the pain of having to roam to and fro over the earth in search of her. In this frame of mind I set myself to prayer.

After a month had passed I thought God was a little slow. After a year I thought him deaf. After three years I believed him positively antagonistic to my cause. He would persist in changing the subject. Every time I asked him for my 'Wonder Woman' he insisted on asking me when I was going to obey him and apply for the ministry. The Holy Spirit answered my prayers with uncomfortable words like, 'Seek first the kingdom of God, and all these things shall be added unto you.' At last I applied to Spurgeon's College and they accepted me for entrance in a year's time. This proved to be God's time for testing me and proving himself. Satan stepped in and provided me with the opportunity of a non-Christian girl-friend. I drifted into this relationship, passing gradually from casual acquaintance to emotional involvement, and a duplicity came into my attitude to prayer. I knew I was doing wrong. I yearned to seek God's face for forgiveness and for assurance that he understood the pressure I was under and therefore was not too disapproving. But I also shied away from him in fear of what he might say. God was good to me. I was able to keep up some kind of devotional life but much of that unfettered openness in prayer was lost. Then God took a hand in the situation by removing the girl. Much to my chagrin she got another boy friend. After a while I was thankful to God as I reaped again the joys of an untainted prayer life.

I continued to besiege God with hopes and visions of matrimonial bliss. I tried twisting his arm a little. I would pray, 'Lord, you know I have obeyed you by applying for the ministry. Budding Baptist ministers are not like Roman Catholic priests, and need wives. I have done my part, so would you kindly do yours?' He had a ready reply from Scripture: 'I have learned, in whatsoever state I am, therewith to be content.' At first I thought this was not playing the game, but I gradually came to acknowledge something that is fundamental to Christian discipleship and prayer. I learned that intercession must be carried out in thankfulness and not in a rebellious or dissatisfied spirit. I knew it was impossible to fight God, for he intended to remain in control of my life. I asked God to work in me so that I was more ready to accept his way, whatever it might be. He helped me to agree to serve him in the ministry and remain single all my life, if that was his will. I found a great release in prayer which compensated for much of the loneliness I felt.

Six months after I had yielded to the Lord on this matter, I met Anne who has now been my wife for fourteen wonderful years. We knew that our relationship was of the Lord from the beginning. I, who had found it so difficult to ask a girl out, now had to cope with an equally embarrassing moment as I knocked on the study door of Dr George Beasley-Murray, Principal of Spurgeon's College, to inform him of my engagement.

'I don't think I've met the young lady at college. How long have you known her?' he asked.

'Oh, about four weeks,' I replied, trying to summon an air of coolness.

This brought a furrow to his brow that no complexity of Greek or Hebrew had ever been able to produce.

'Four weeks!'

'Yes, sir.'

He thought for a little and then said with a kind smile, 'Well, I don't suppose I can tell a man of thirty what to do, can I?'

Anne was only twenty-one then. I could hardly have gone out with her eight years earlier! I learned humbly that God knew what he was doing all those years, and that when I prayed I must allow him to answer in his own way in his own time. I try to remember this as I cope with the strains of pastoral ministry and seek to bring people and issues before God.

The Child of Promise

Most people go into marriage hoping for a family. Anne and I confidently awaited the arrival of the children we believed God had promised us. I managed to pick up a bargain pram from a Christian friend. After two years that pram was dismantled and accumulating dust in the loft. After three years the thought of it being anywhere in the house was so painful that we considered selling it or giving it away. We continued to pray for strength to accept God's will. I had learned to wait for God's best when praying for a wife but it still wasn't easy to maintain the prayer of faith. We asked many questions. Why should God give us a child when many Christian couples had to remain childless? Were we mistaken in the assumption that God had promised us children? Hadn't we met plenty of immature fanatics claiming this, that, and the other from God and then coming to grief? Were we any different? We had a good marriage. We were complete in the Lord as we were. Why not be satisfied? Wouldn't we be more free to serve the Lord without the demands made by children? In fact we were not dissatisfied. Discontent has always had more to do with my attitude to God than with my circumstances. Something indefinable kept us praying. I now know it was the Lord, but I was not always so sure then.

After about three years we both attended the Fertility

Clinic at Saint Thomas' Hospital. The report was extremely discouraging. We were both sub-fertile, and short of a miracle we would be unlikely to have any children. Now we had the truth there was little option but to pray for healing though recent events had not encouraged us to do that. Anne's father had not long before died from cancer of the jaw. He had suffered a lingering painful death. His face had been scorched with radium, and half his upper jaw had been removed. We had prayed, but there had been no healing. In spite of all this we could not stop praying. We were not desperate. Sometimes I did not pray about it for a month, but then I would return to it. How wonderful it is when the Spirit aids our prayers. He gives us a peace and patience we could never have in ourselves. He brings his mighty purposes to fruition through the stuttering prayers of his children.

About a year later Anne went to our GP for a pregnancy test. This was never easy for her as there had been several negative results over the years. She could not bring herself to phone in for the result. I had to do it, but then had the joy of breaking to her the news that it was positive. The next few months had their difficulties and Anne was admitted to hospital for bed rest. I was present at the birth. It was a boy. We called him Jonathan because it means 'The Lord gives'.

When Jonathan was little more than six months old my wife suspected that she was pregnant again. Her joy over the first child was turned to anger about a second. This was not what we had planned. It was too much of a good thing. How would we cope with two children so close together? When we calmed down enough to pray about it properly, we suddenly saw how completely God had healed us and that this was his way of showing it. Then we were able to laugh, but we still felt that the Lord had made too good a job of it. Fourteen months after the birth of Jonathan, David (the 'girl' we decided we wanted) duly arrived. These two boys were great friends from the beginning. When we moved to Streatham there were no young children living in our street. Without David, Jonathan would have been solitary. God knew that all the time. I believe in prayer because of the perfect timing of God's answers. Sometimes I think he's taking too long, and he does not always give me what I want, but it all works out right too many times for it to be mere coincidence.

From Paint to Pastorate

I did not find the transition from paint chemistry to pastoral ministry very easy. Part of me still yearns for the predictability of mathematical formulation. With well documented records, slide-rule, thermometer and a bit of patience I could normally get what I was after. I meet some ministers who are looking for a formula to put the church right. Why are people so obstinate or variable? Why don't they respond like tins of paint? I would try something and it often produced the opposite of what I intended. Then there was an invisible, intangible God working behind the scenes and I couldn't always see what he was doing or where he was going. I was no longer the calculating scientist, but had to take the humble position of servant, schoolboy and son.

I now know that God often takes us right to the end of the road before he answers our prayer. There I am, standing in a cul-de-sac and he shows me a narrow alley between two buildings which leads to a new road. There is Abraham having to wait until Sarah is past the age of child-bearing before God gave him Isaac. There is Samuel at Bethlehem scratching his head, having seen seven sons of Jesse and drawn a blank on every one. He does not know that God has the eighth away in the fields keeping the sheep. I have prayed, even agonised, over some of the flock of God. The more I prayed the worse they seemed to get. Or, even more frustrating, someone takes one step forward followed by ten steps backward. Then I tell the Lord I've had enough. I shall tell the deacons I'm resigning and joining the dole queue. He then tells me I ought to be thankful to have a job today, with the best boss in the world at that. I have to agree and get on with it. I can often see where the flesh and the devil are busy in a tough situation, but it takes persistent prayer to find the all-important thing: where is the Lord? He has promised to be there, and he is there. He is not interested in slick, superficial answers in dealing with people and churches. The answer can be a long time coming sometimes because God has more to do with the person than answering the immediate prayer, sometimes because the person or church is resisting his will. In the latter case he is forced to bring us down a longer and harder road than should have been necessary.

A pastor can rejoice in God's ability to 'work all things together for good for those who love him'. For the most resistant there is still grace, so we can always pray and love. Recently I felt helpless to oversee every family and individual in the church. As I prayed God gave me a promise from scripture: 'He tends his flock like a shepherd: He gathers the lambs in his arms and carries them close to his heart; he gently leads those that have young' (Isaiah 40.11). He was also reminding me that he is the great shepherd over the household of God. I am the under-shepherd. I must be faithful but will over-reach myself if I try to take on his job also. It is my privilege to pray to him concerning situations I can't deal with.

God has never failed me since I made my first tentative steps twenty years ago to follow his call to preach the word. Most of my preaching has come directly out of my prayer life. I have never deliberately used my quiet time to cull sermons for Sundays. However God has often shown me what to bring to others as I have had a devotional soak in a passage of scripture. He shows me more treasures from his word if I am desirous of passing them on to others. I am hesitant to preach a sermon to others, if God has not spoken to me through it first. I no longer feel guilty if I stop praying and write it down. Sometimes I used to feel that this was cheating God out of prayer time, and when I got tired or tense it was because I was not praying enough. One day God showed me that tiredness and tension are usually due to guilt or dissatisfaction. Sometimes I have not been grateful enough to God for what he has given me in prayer, unwittingly entertaining proud visions of myself as a prince of prayer spending hours with the Lord. I was not able to grow in prayer because I was so negative about what I had already. While it was essential to spend time alone with God, I was not to see this as an escape from the world, an oasis in the desert, or even a table in the wilderness. My prayer life was to be related to the glory of serving God here on earth also. This came home to me when I met pastors who spent much time in prayer, but found it difficult to feed the flock every Sunday. I must not lose the simple expectancy that God will give me sermons; I must not look for super-spiritual ways of provision and so miss his way of providing for me as I am now.

Anyone, Anywhere, Any Time, Anything

Good books are written on the necessity of prayer, the power of prayer, the lack of prayer, prayer warfare and the like. Can anyone tell me of a volume on 'the simple delights of prayer' written by an evangelical today? We tend to make things complicated and difficult. The top professionals perform to perfection while we sit passively watching them on a television screen. Only the gifted few have anything to offer. Our society is in danger of polarising between those who commit themselves totally and those who 'cop out'. This must not be allowed to happen in the realm of prayer. Anyone can pray. Even the dumb can talk to the Lord. Even the deaf can hear his voice. In prayer we can be ourselves as nowhere else. For this reason I have chosen to write about my prayer pilgrimage in areas very central to my life and being. Some of these areas are common to most of us. As you pray through them Jesus will lead you along a different path from mine, but it will be as right for you as it has been for me. One of my sons entertains the thought of becoming a professional cricketer. He is mad on David Gower. In moments of fantasy he dresses up in whites, bat, pads and gloves. Blond-haired and left-handed, he looks the image of his hero. Yet if he ever achieves his exalted ambition he will do so only as himself, and not as a carbon copy of another, however famous and gifted that other might be.

I have found it important in prayer to find my own level and seek to progress from there. My foster daughter Emily has been swimming for seven months. By sheer hard work and determination she has fought initial co-ordination problems and can already swim 800 metres, but she cannot keep up with Jonathan. The more she used to try, the less she enjoyed her swimming and she lost all appreciation of what she had achieved. The prowess of her brother had spurred her on in the early stages, but she got things out of balance and could have given up altogether. Happily, we took it to the Lord and he resolved it for us.

For me, private prayer is delightful conversation with a loving Father and a trusted friend. It is the most intimate and personal area of my walk with God. It is the simplest thing in the Christian life. As a baby learns to communicate with its mother from birth, so any child of God may talk to his Father in heaven. My prayer life will involve deeper and more responsible matters as I mature in Christ, but I know that when I have allowed these to oust the simple joy of the 'Thou-I' relationship things go wrong.

I believe in prayer because I have a mind, a heart, a tongue and a God. I must never put up a false front with God. In prayer I can only be myself even at my worst. What is the point of pretence when he knows the truth anyway?

I believe in prayer because Jesus is always available: any time, anywhere. As a child I had to wait for father to come home from work. It is not like that with God. I know I must not rob him of those times when I must shut out everything else and give him my full attention, but I can also talk to him while I work. Conversation is a great help in a tedious or unpleasant job. My own father was a good listener, but he was human and would sometimes sigh or snap, 'Don't bother me with that!' In prayer I can share whatever is on my mind and gain a hearing. I may think it too futile or too embarrassing to confide in anyone, but God will listen. I am often helped by these famous lines by J. M. Scriven:

> What a friend we have in Jesus,
>   All our sins and griefs to bear.
> What a privilege to carry
>   Everything to God in prayer.

God refers to Abraham as 'my friend' (Isaiah 41.8). I am a spiritual descendant of Abraham through faith, and so share the joys of friendship with God. The life of prayer is fully comprehensive, embracing the heights of heaven and the depths of my sinful humanity. I can enter into purposes of the Almighty which are far bigger than myself and my times, and share things which appear to my fellow men as of less substance than a sparrow. In friendship it doesn't always matter what you talk about. Conversation is a convenient excuse for being together. The miracle of prayer is that I can talk to my Maker.

Recently a ninety-four year old servant of God, the Rev Harry Brown, went home to his Lord. The family kindly allowed me to take my pick from his bookshelf. I chanced upon a faded red volume, *Praying Hyde – The Official Life – A Challenge to Prayer*. I thought, 'Dare I?' and then, 'Why not?' It was immediately clear that John Hyde was no Napoleon, Bradman, or Beethoven. I read, 'At first John Hyde was not a remarkable missionary. He was slow of speech. When a question or a remark was directed to him he seemed not to hear, or if he heard he seemed a long time in framing a reply. His hearing was slightly defective and this it was feared would hinder him from acquiring the language. His disposition was gentle and quiet: he seemed to be lacking in the enthusiasm and zeal which a young missionary should have. He had a wonderful pair of blue eyes . . . .'

Ah! Human after all. But God accomplished extraordinary things because this very ordinary servant gave prayer the highest priority. It is the same for all other ordinary Christians. We may not have the anointing for intercession that was on John Hyde, but we can all talk directly to God anywhere, any time and about any-thing.

I believe in prayer because I believe in God.

Elaine Brown

Prayer: Strength in Weakness

Settling in Aberdeenshire has brought its own particular pleasure since, prior to 1977, I'd always been on the move. Born in Burma, and brought up elsewhere abroad, life had been full of varied interest and pleasure. But now Scotland has become a valued home.

Following our return as a family to Britain I've had time for writing, and the development of this serious hobby has proved fulfilling, if sometimes frustrating. Involvement in the life of our village and kirk is also a pleasurable challenge; then there's always our growing family (and an eccentric cat) to further keep me on my toes.

It has been during our time here, in this quiet and beautiful northern setting, that God has chosen to weave many unexpected threads into the fabric of our everyday lives.

'If God loves us why has he allowed things to go so wrong?' – a question most despairing people ask over and over again. We've struggled for a long time with it too, only gradually to learn that the Lord has unexpected ways of satisfying such deep bewilderment. Prayer has had an important part to play in this learning experience, being mostly a desperate cry for help but sometimes a means by which we've hesitantly opened ourselves up more to God. And then? Well, maybe I should share the whole story.

Four years ago we were happy and content, full of gratitude for the many good things the Lord had given us. After some years of missionary work in Africa our family had returned to live in the Aberdeen area where my husband, Les, had obtained a promising position as captain with a national airline. Our daughter and twin sons, just into their teens, were well settled at school, and we were all glad to be living in this beautiful northern countryside.

Then, one bitterly cold winter's night, Les came in from a late flight, his face grim. Everything about him filled me with sudden apprehension. What was wrong? Speaking slowly, Les broke the news: he'd lost his job. It seemed impossible. I just couldn't believe what he was trying to tell me. But later, as we sat quietly together by the fireside, the truth began to press against my mind. How *could* this have happened? What were we going to do? The basis of our happy, secure world had collapsed, throwing everything else into jeopardy. That night, helpless and crushed by circumstances, we knelt together and tried to tell Jesus how we felt, asking him to provide Les with another opening soon. Our prayers seemed rather mechanical, but it was one constructive thing we could do in the midst of our confusion. After we'd gone to bed foreboding gripped my mind. Was this the first ominous hint of much more to follow? Were we about to enter the cold darkness of a long, bleak tunnel? I tried in vain to shake off this fear but eventually grew too tired to fight it. Somewhere after midnight I fell asleep.

Over the next few weeks I attempted to keep things running smoothly at home while struggling inwardly with the implications of what had happened. As I swept snow from the doorstep or tackled a high pile of ironing I'd share a long request list with Jesus: 'Please help Les to cope. Please give me the right words to say, and show me how to comfort him. Please give new employment soon, and meanwhile keep us from becoming bitter.'

Although Jesus already knew our different needs it was helpful to list and then commit them specifically to him. Doing so restored some order to my thinking. But when I was overtired, or when Les received another 'no' to the numerous job enquiries he was making, fear would push in again and I'd start to grab back the worries deliberately handed over to the Lord earlier on. Later I would feel ashamed and ask for forgiveness. It was at such times of acute self-disapproval that I discovered the extreme tenderness of the Lord. He wasn't standing over me pointing the finger. He took my frailty into account and was waiting to restore peace as soon as I was able to receive it. That discovery has been very important to me over these years.

Weeks became months. Les was still without work. We didn't grow used to the situation but when the first shock had eased we gradually found ways of coping. I recognised that the Lord *had* been answering my prayers. Les was managing to keep outwardly cheerful and this wasn't just a mask for others to see. He was able to give himself to times of genuine fun with friends and family, particularly enjoying a good 'bundle' on the living-room floor with one of our lads. (What loud shrieks of delight!) Jesus was also showing me how to be more sensitive to my husband's inner feelings and reactions. I was learning to affirm my confidence in Les rather than offer endless ideas and suggestions. Then, too, there were many ways in which to show simple, practical caring. I'd make Les one of his favourite meals, or pack a spur of the moment picnic to enjoy together in nearby hills. Sometimes we'd walk along the river bank beyond our house and watch a brave dipper darting into the ice-clear water from his safe rock perch, or scan the far woods for a first faint haze of green. In all these different ways God helped us to become more positive.

Over the next eighteen months Les obtained various temporary labouring jobs. He sorted potatoes, cut steel cables, and cleaned workshop machinery. As I watched him lacing his thick-soled boots or gathering up old overalls it seemed impossible that only the previous year he'd been at the controls of a passenger prop-jet.

Another summer was approaching. 'Airlines will be recruiting now!' Les told me. But as the warm sunlit months passed and autumn came there was still no work, despite a couple of interviews. The whole experience became irksome in the extreme. 'What is God trying to say to us in all of this?' we kept asking, but there was no obvious answer. Watching Les, I became aware of his increasing sense of uselessness and failure and I yearned to relieve him, even to bear the pain instead. The hardest part of all was to see Les' anguish, while being helpless to take it from him. 'Lord, please give him work soon,' I pleaded. 'Or if it isn't to be soon, then hold tightly to him through all of this. Don't let him give up in despair.'

That September Les was invited to help ferry an old Dakota aircraft across to Florida, USA. He loves Dakotas and jumped at the opportunity, thoroughly enjoying the unusual flight. The aircraft had been purchased by a mission group operating from West Palm Beach and a few months later they made contact again. 'Would Les like to help them out for six months?' I was glad because this was work Les most enjoyed, but I was hesitant about a lengthy separation and my ability to meet financial needs during his absence. Les' visitor's visa meant working on a voluntary basis, and we would not qualify for unemployment benefit once he left Britain.

Another Christmas came. As before, our neighbours and friends showed unusual kindness and we were amazed by their thoughtfulness. It humbled us to be on the receiving end of such generosity. Quite suddenly I recognised what the Lord was trying to show me. Had he failed us over the two long years since Les had lost his job? Had we lacked anything we needed? The answer was a clear-cut 'no'. In fact we'd been blessed in numerous unexpected ways. Well then, couldn't I trust the Lord now, and for the next six months? I drew back, uncertain. It seemed such a big thing, so I stalled for a few days and concentrated on the busy school holidays instead.

The new year brought several letters and cheques from unexpected quarters. People (some complete strangers) had heard about the Florida job and wanted to stand by us financially so that Les could leave, as proposed, in mid-January. Within days we had enough pledged income to cover the first three months, with more funds promised. It was obviously right for Les to go, though the parting was hard. We had been so close to one another during this period of unemployment. Now we would need to face new challenges alone. Little did we realise how vital those months were to prove in restoring Les' confidence.

The Lord answers our requests in such intriguing ways! I'd asked for 'permanent work soon' and he'd given Les temporary work almost immediately, but so far away. Why? Looking back now I can see why the Lord planned it that way. He wanted to turn our personal loneliness into valuable 'aloneness' with himself, so that we would be brought closer to God and to one another. We would need that deepening three-way oneness in the harder circumstances which still lay ahead.

The next six months went quite well. The knowledge that Les was busy and fulfilled in a worthwhile flying programme helped to offset the sadness of his absence, though sometimes it was hard to see his empty chair at the meal table or to go up to a dark empty room at night. As winter became spring I experienced a growing inner fear. This became a constant weight pressing on my mind, in contrast to previous temporary episodes of acute apprehension. When the pressure reached a pitch I'd escape to our bedroom and sink into the large old armchair which was becoming a valued refuge. Then I'd sit and gaze out at the far beeches, seeing their widespread branches calmly brushing against the sky, listening for the river's murmuring or the occasional cry of an oyster-catcher. The steady, ordered ongoing of the world outside would start to seep into my turmoiled thinking and with it would come a growing awareness of Christ's presence, his unhurried calm, his dependability. I was troubled yet he remained always the same. Though he knew every detail of the future there was no tension in him. As I leant further back into the comfort of that big armchair I could sense the reality of leaning back against Jesus, feeling the safety of his protection. I began to realise that there was no need to try and work up the necessary faith myself so that Christ could then recognise and reward it. *Everything* is his gift to us – from the first hesitant desire and reaching out, to the eventual relief of leaning back fully into all that he waits to be.

Les returned in July. It was so good to be together again! Now, with the asset of recent flying experience, he was full of renewed confidence. This was justified three months later when a small British airline offered him a promising opening as captain on their Bandereinte aircraft. We were absolutely delighted! It was our answer at last! The whole family joined in the excitement and while Les packed, I booked his plane ticket south for that Thursday afternoon.

Within hours of his planned departure the phone rang. Our doctor had received results from recent tests he'd advised for Les. A degenerative neck condition had been diagnosed which could be controlled by drugs but not cured. Whether receiving treatment or not, the Civil

Aviation authorities had confirmed that Les would be precluded from holding a pilot's licence. He would not be able to fly again.

We were stunned by this news. It was such a bitter blow for Les. Why had it come just as he was starting that long-awaited job? What *was* God trying to tell us? 'To look in a completely new direction' was the answer friends might have suggested, but they weren't to know how overwhelming this reversal was for Les. His whole career had come to an end. It was gone. I shall never forget the empty silence of that day. There was nothing to say, only a whole new set of bewildering circumstances to try and grasp. But we couldn't grasp them. At first we couldn't even pray.

A week passed. Les forced himself to draw up new plans in his search for work. It was a hard discipline, for his heart was still in flying and he had no other qualifications. We were particularly aware of our friends' support at this stage. We were often too tired and bewildered to put our thoughts into prayers, but we knew others were putting arms of prayer around us, keeping us in the presence of Christ. This was vital. When people half-apologised with 'We wish we could do more than just pray,' I'd immediately think, '*Just* pray?'

Then as another year ended a friend passed on an advertisement for an assistant warden's position at a conference centre in central Scotland. We followed it up straight away and in January Les was invited for an interview. There was a growing 'rightness' about the possibility, and when Les was asked to attend a second interview we really became excited. This *was* it! The Lord had caused Les' flying career to end precisely so that he could then lead us into this new ministry. Everything was fitting so perfectly together and I felt justified in predicting the Lord's answer this time, though I hesitated to be too vocal about it. The second interview went well, Les and one other man now being the only candidates under consideration. 'And both of you are equally well suited to the work,' Les was told. We were promised an answer within days. It came a week later. The other fellow had been appointed to the post.

You never get used to disappointments. Each is even harder than the last. How many more could Les take? How much longer could we keep going? Why had God allowed this opportunity to seem so right only to sweep it away just when we were poised to take it up?

'Lord, we can't make sense out of anything any more,' I remember crying aloud. 'Please just keep us holding on to you in this frightening new darkness.'

It was several days before Les could bring himself to start the search all over again. Where should he try now? Where could we even begin? Various agencies in the city promised to keep Les under consideration and we also contacted the home office of the mission with which we'd worked in Africa. They were interested and invited Les down for a visit.

A few days later an agency offered him a temporary portering job at the large BP complex near Aberdeen, so he took this while we carefully considered a proposed move south. Les had also filled in an application form for permanent work in the gas flow department at BP and we were happily surprised when he was given an interview in early April. The result would be posted to us in due course.

Since the new year I'd had a few bouts of unpleasant abdominal pain. Gallstones were diagnosed and just after Les' BP interview I was due to have an operation. It was a difficult time for both of us. I was apprehensive about the surgery and Les, whilst getting physically tired from his busy portering job, was also tussling with two contrasting work possibilities (the mission or BP). The night before my admission to hospital we knelt together beside the bed and poured out our thoughts in prayer. 'And, Lord, please could you give us a definite answer from BP by the end of the month, 30th April?' Les added. Too bewilderd to keep trying to work things out for ourselves, we'd agreed to set a deadline and ask the Lord to clearly order our circumstances prior to that date. If BP said 'yes' we'd stay, if their answer was 'no' we'd feel at ease about moving south. Once we might have hesitated to operate to such a rigid ruling but now we were losing confidence in our ability to discern the Lord's purpose. Would he mind spelling it out for us in this clear-cut way? We felt sure he wouldn't. He so completely understood our frustration.

It was hard to go through with that operation and the long convalescence which followed. I wanted to be active and well, able to support and encourage Les. Instead it had to be the other way round. Again that so-important leaning back became vital to my wellbeing, and during those slow weeks I came to experience even more of Christ's tenderness. Sometimes it was as if he was bending close and whispering, 'Just lie back further still. Give me those anxious, tired thoughts. Then I can comfort you, putting my calm where all your frustration has been.' It was such a real, practical concern, experienced directly in those moments of silent relinquishment with Jesus and also in the many touches of kindness with which friends ministered to me. All was the tenderness of God.

Our 30th April deadline – a Saturday – arrived. There had been no word from BP. I was still convalescing, so Les got up to prepare breakfast, but before he went downstairs we stopped for a shared Bible reading and prayer.

'Lord, please give us an answer today!' Les asked.

At nine o'clock I heard the door flap click. Les went to collect the mail. There *was* a letter from BP! It began, 'We have pleasure . . .' Oh, what *joy*, they were offering Les a permanent job at last! We were so elated that we almost forgot about breakfast, and feeding the cat. What a day of celebration followed! It meant so much to have good news to tell family and friends. The mission leaders were pleased for us too, sharing the conviction that in this opening God had definitely supplied our much-needed answer.

Just before Les' brief training period began we spent a few days away on the Morayshire coast, by way of celebration. What a glorious May weekend! Everything was fresh and vibrant in the gleaming sunlight – gorse blooms gold along the narrow lanes, larches a pale trembling green, wood anemones scattered like white stars in the soft new grass. One afternoon we visited Pluscarden Abbey, set in a quiet valley south of Findhorn Bay. We arrived as prayers were starting and sat in the side chapel listening to the solemn plainsong which rose to echo through the high stone arches. What a magnificent sound! What a sense of being in the holy grandeur of God's presence. Was this the same Lord who had whispered so gently to me in those troubled moments just a month earlier? I knew it was. And he was with us still, even as we came out of the long darkness into the joyous sunlight of a whole new pathway.

By now I was much stronger and keen to be back in action. Our northern world was eagerly responding to summer's warmth and gaiety and, matching the mood, our hearts were full of confident happiness. One sunlit afternoon I drove to the hospital for a routine post-operative check, knowing, with such a sense of relief, that this would be my last visit as everything had gone so well. The surgeon walked slowly into the clinic cubicle and pulled a chair up beside the couch. 'I'm sorry,' he began gently, 'but a small liver growth found at the operation has proved to be malignant. I'll need to take some more tissue away, just as a safeguard.' His words came as a deep shock, particularly because I'd been so full of confidence. My mind suddenly began to reel and I could feel tears pricking my eyes. I hardly knew how to walk back to the car. Where had I left it? How would I get home? And all the while the sun was still shining from a clear, gleaming sky. The diagnosis couldn't be true. It just couldn't. Not now, when everything had started to come so right for us.

What do you do at times like that? What do you think, or say, or pray? I don't know. Everything is confused and unreal. You cannot function in an ordered, logical way. You simply live from moment to moment, constantly trying to convince yourself that everything is a mistake.

But it wasn't a mistake. For all those previous months I had watched Les' suffering and anguish. Now I was entering into a similar experience myself. It was overwhelming. Yet during those first few days I remember being comforted by the realisation that Jesus was still very close to me despite my distress. Now, though, I was too troubled to relax and linger with him as I had once done in the stillness of our upstairs bedroom. In gentleness he made up for this by offering me sudden unexpected moments of reassurance, concentrating what he wanted to give me into the brief times when I was able to respond. One such occasion occurred two days later when I was still very shocked. Returning from the village shops, I found a bouquet of yellow and white spray carnations on the kitchen table. They'd been left by Sally, a busy young mum who had been through difficult times too. I was very touched by her kindness and deliberately took a long time arranging those flowers. Each one was so complete, so perfect! As I lingered over them I couldn't help being drawn to the Lord in wondering appreciation for they reflected him so clearly. The worship of those few moments brought important inner stillness and refreshment.

Gradually I was able to accept what had happened, but I just couldn't face the thought of another operation, particularly now that there was a sinister aspect to the problem. I tried to reassure myself by recalling the surgeon's words, 'It is only a small growth and isn't likely to spread', but then the word 'cancer' would break into my thinking again, giving access to all kinds of fears.

One afternoon I lay down on the settee, longing for relief, and began to ask Christ about healing. Could he do this? Would he? How wonderful to experience such a miracle! I'd be able to forget all about the hospital and the operation. Surely healing must be his purpose for me? I paused for a while, watching swallows and swifts skimming the shining sky. Then, unmistakably, I sensed Jesus' inner voice.

'Can't you accept? Can't you just rest it all with me so that I can go with you through each part of this hard experience and even turn it to some value?'

I lay very still, struggling to be willing to see the matter from this totally different angle. 'Lord, please help me to be open to an alternative,' I said. 'Please help me to want to see it your way.'

I had hardly known how to share the news with Les. He'd said little (he rarely does at such moments) but I sensed he was feeling with me, not merely for me. Just as I had once tried to share his suffering, so now he was trying to share mine. It was a poignant yet valuable bond. It was also difficult, even embarrassing, to mention the matter to friends. Weeks earlier they had so fully shared our joy over the BP job. Now I could almost read their thoughts. 'Why has God allowed this to happen just when everything was going so well?' I didn't know why, only that, despite my inner questioning, I needed to take refuge in Jesus. In this way I could still find safety.

In those June days we were living with such contrasts. Les' new work began during the first week. It was a big red-letter occasion and I determined that nothing must overshadow the gladness of a parting kiss and wave that first morning. Then came the eager waiting for Les' return at six o'clock. As soon as he reached the door we all swamped him with questions.

'Yes, the day went very well!' Les reported, smiling at the bombardment.

Our family prayers around the supper table were full of 'thank yous' and this shared happiness offset my own carefully camouflaged apprehension. 'Lord, thank you just for *this* day!' I remember saying later. It was easier to cope if I concentrated on the immediacy of 'now' rather than struggling with an endless succession of unknown tomorrows.

Two days after Les started work I was admitted to hospital. The operation went well but left me in a very weak condition. During the first few post-operative days it meant so much when Les or another visitor stopped to pray briefly with me. The pain and apprehension receded a little and I felt refreshed, like being given a long sip of cool water. There were also times when fear about my illness grew to large, unmanageable proportions. I tried to fight back but was too weak and vulnerable. Eventually my mind just cried out 'Jesus!' and for the moment this brought relief.

Eventually, when I was allowed home, these battles with acute fear eased. I was able to lie back in the quiet bedroom and it was then that the Lord began to open my mind again to beauty and worship. There was one particular summer's evening when, while listening to Vivaldi's beautiful 'Four Seasons', I watched the changing sky: intense scarlet and gold, then deepening blue pierced by a single rising star. The world outside was so still (only the poplar leaves trembled), so rich with the glory of God. Everything within me longed to respond to such a magnificent Lord. I began to reach out beyond immediate circumstances, beyond the lingering sadness, to discover him in a totally new way. It is hard to adequately fit such an experience into words. I only know that in those moments I found him, not so much as an awesome Creator, nor even as a familiar Helper, but as Christ *belonging* to me, never until then so fully recognised and delighted in. No longer need it be a matter of trying to live for him, but *out* of him. What a magnificent truth this is! I have marvelled at it so many times since, eager to prove more of its reality.

This living out of Christ, consciously drawing on his resources for each day's varied experiences, has at last released me from the tight grip of fear. For a while after the second operation I evaded the issue of cancer, trying to convince myself that the problem had only been a small, insignificant thing. But the convincing never quite succeeded. Then, with the help of a doctor, I was able to recognise that although the growth had been treated early, I must accept the necessity of regular check-ups because a recurrence could not be categorically ruled out. Initially, confrontation with this fact triggered apprehension, but then a few friends offered help by coming to pray and lay hands on me. Together we committed my illness to the Lord, affirming our confidence in his greater wisdom and power. This marked a turning point. The grip of fear was finally broken and although I have been tempted by it since, the effect is only temporary. Fear about cancer doesn't live constantly within me any longer.

Now I'm free to eagerly think and plan for the future. We really have started out along a whole new pathway! Les' work is going well ('He's a different person now!' friends often comment) and, with the slow return of strength, there are all kinds of things I'm waiting to do.

'What have you learnt most through all that has happened?' people sometimes ask.

'We've learnt that God is utterly good!' Once we struggled with so many baffling 'whys', yet now he has made our questioning lose significance when compared to his unfailing tenderness and understanding. He has offered us so much – strength for weakness, comfort for sorrow, victory for defeat and, above all else, more and more of himself, the 'I in you and you in me' which Jesus so vividly described. In wisdom he chose to make all of this real through prolonged adversity. Perhaps, for us, there was no other way.

Henry Clarke

Prayer: He Can When We Can't

Henry and Verena Clarke have been married ten years and have four children. They live in Harpenden, Herts, where they are members of the Bethany Christian Fellowship. Verena was formerly a teacher in a South London comprehensive school. Henry is a chartered surveyor with a Master's degree in Business Management, and a senior manager with the British Rail Property Board. He is a co-founding member of Praise the Lord Ventures Limited, a Christian charitable company, and he is a national council member of the Christian Union for the Estates Profession. With others, Henry and Verena helped to pioneer a new Christian Fellowship in Wilmslow, Cheshire.

'Jesus himself drew near, and went with them' (Luke 24.15). These were the precious words of Scripture given to us at our marriage service. They speak of a walk with Jesus during which God reveals his perfect will for us. As in any walk in life there are always notable milestones on the way. For us, these mark experiences through which God has underlined the importance of constant companionship with him in prayer.

The disciples on the Emmaus Road found that their hearts burned within them as the risen Lord revealed his purposes through the Scriptures. If we are receptive to the word of God and to the purposes he has for us, then our hearts too will be stirred to respond. Jesus is looking for a heart relationship with himself in prayer. This I learned through an incident while studying for a post graduate degree at London University.

One afternoon, about five years after beginning my professional career with British Rail, one of the directors telephoned me. 'Henry,' he said, 'we've been given a chance to send someone on a year's business study course. Would you like to be considered?' I was surprised to be singled out but excited at the prospect. The interviews were a little daunting, especially when I was advised of the competition for places but eventually I heard that my nomination was accepted and I set out to select the course which I should attend.

I decided to study in London where I could be close to my family – by then we had a five-month-old daughter – and I obtained a place on the Master's degree course at Imperial College. Because I was being sponsored, I was accepted without having to undergo the University's strenuous screening procedure. Then I began to read some of the pre-course literature. It slowly dawned on me that the mathematical content of much of the course was far beyond my capabilities. I'd only studied elementary mathematics to 'O' level. The standard required was at least undergraduate level and I was obviously going to have some fundamental problems. But it was too late to back out.

On day one of the course it registered in my mind that in only nine months I would be examined in seven subjects of which at least three required an advanced understanding and experience of mathematical sciences which I had not got. To my horror, the time of reckoning was to come rather sooner than I'd thought. To sort out the sheep from the goats, all seventy-five entrants were required to sit a maths examination the very next day. The result was predictable—I was bottom of the class! For the next twelve weeks I struggled on, taking sometimes between forty-eight to ninety-six hours on single assignments which most other course members could do in less than an hour.

I was getting nowhere, becoming thoroughly depressed and almost frantic. My difficulties were beginning to affect the rest of my course work. I became irritable, impatient and unreasonable. I tried every remedy possible, but to no avail. More than once I was ready to give up, though to do so could have cost me my career. If this was what business management was about, I wanted none of it.

Then God intervened. My wife, Verena, and I had realised that it would be important for us as a family to get away for a few days over the New Year. We booked in at a Christian holiday and conference centre in the West Country. There God began to challenge me particularly about my prayer life. What sort of relationship had I got with him that I could not share the burden which had almost broken me? Didn't I know that with God all things are possible (Matthew 19.26) and that in everything Jesus has purpose and victory? Didn't the Lord Jesus Christ live in me? Had he not given me hope through the power of the Holy Spirit for everything needed in life?

'Yes, Lord, you have given me power in your name for these things, but I now know that I need to reach out and take hold of that power, to be filled with your Holy Spirit, to walk with you in a new 'heart to heart' relationship of trusting and obedience.' Almost at once God put a sense of peace and joy in my heart. I realised that he had wanted to help me all along and had wanted to converse with me, like father and son, but I hadn't had the humility to admit my failure to God. I had called out often in despair and prayed those 'arrow' prayers, but now God wanted me to walk with him in a new spiritual dimension. The Lord Jesus gave me a new strength and purpose and set the Holy Spirit within me so that *we* could deal with the problems I faced.

Jesus was utterly faithful to the commitment I had made in prayer to him. I found renewed power and strength in my prayer life. The Lord expected me to continue working under pressure and he does now in my business life, but the difference is that he gives the strength to cope in situations where without him I would inevitably fail.

In due course I sat the examinations. It wasn't God's purpose to make me a mathematician but as a result of my perseverance and faith in his promises I passed the most difficult examination by a single mark – that was God's mark on my life.

In every aspect of our Emmaus walk with Jesus, he desires to reveal his purposes for us. Knowing that Jesus is Lord in my own life and believing that his Holy Spirit dwells within me, I could walk no other way. I share with him every decision at home, in the family, in business and in the fellowship of his people. It has become my daily practice to talk with my Father about the plans for that day's business and to ask for his help so that I am aware of his presence in all I do. Important decisions to be taken at work I share first with Jesus and I often ask Verena for prayer support. I have found that the most difficult and potentially impossible business problems are miraculously resolved, not because of my own efforts but because I've laid them before God. 'Everything is possible for him who believes' Jesus says (Mark 9.23). I learned that believing should be a continuous, not just an occasional, reliance on him. My prayer life must reflect an ever deepening love, awareness and companionship with the Lord involving a heart relationship and understanding. The words of Joseph Scriven, who knew much despair and suffering, are a testimony to this privileged relationship we have with God in prayer:

What a friend we have in Jesus,
  All our sins and griefs to bear.
What a privilege to carry
  Everything to God in prayer.
O what peace we often forfeit,
  O what needless pain we bear,
All because we do not carry
  Everything to God in prayer.

Having established a true heart relationship with God we can move on to fulfil God's purpose in our lives. If we respond to the promptings of the Holy Spirit then God will give us a desire and a persistence in intercession for those matters that are of real concern to him. Sometimes these prayers are very specific. Often several people will have a similar burden to pray for a particular issue. It is as if the foundations of the work God wants us to do need to be dug by prayers. We must go on digging in order to establish a solid and lasting foundation.

When God moved us to Wilmslow about a year after my course in business studies, he gave us a burden to pray for the town. We had come north in response to a promotional challenge in my job. I had no knowledge of the place in which I was to work and we knew no one in the Manchester area. God specifically directed us to look for a house in Wilmslow, a town just twelve miles south of Manchester. When it took only one weekend to find a house, survey it, make an offer and have lunch with the vendors, our belief that God wanted us there for a purpose was confirmed.

Before we moved, I went to Wilmslow and toured the churches on foot. I was looking for something to tell me that there was a lively church in the area. Nowhere could I find signs of life — no posters or welcome notices to tell me that Jesus was alive and well and living in Wilmslow. We were even more disheartened when we came to visit the churches after we had moved. We also discovered that the powers of darkness had had a stranglehold over the town and its neighbouring village of Alderley Edge for far too long. Witchcraft and occult practices abounded while comparative wealth made many complacent towards God.

There was some encouragement, however. A group of Christians met mid-week for prayer, praise and fellowship in the local Guide hut. They came together from nearly every church in the town, sensing the need to be uplifted and to pray for their own church situations. We also met another couple who shared the same burden for the town, and learned from them that two attempts had been made in the past to start a new, thoroughly Bible-based, evangelistic work there. The four of us often prayed together, sometimes having Sunday worship in our home. God began to reveal to us that we were to prepare ourselves for something new: 'See, I am doing a new thing' (Isaiah 43.19). Bearing in mind the previous failed attempts, we realised the kind of battles we could expect. We sent out letters to all those we thought would be interested, explaining what God had placed on our hearts and asking for their prayers as we sought God's will. The letters were followed up with a meeting in our house. It was a great encouragement to discover that some elderly ladies had been praying over several years for just such a venture. In this way, we believe, the earth had been cleared and Wilmslow made ready for the foundations to be dug in anticipation of a fresh move of God's Spirit in the people.

Just on the boundary between Wilmslow and Alderley Edge, the members of a little chapel were preparing to close its doors. Only six, on average, attended for just the one evening service per week. Numbers were falling, church services were suspended for two months of the year, and the financial situation didn't look promising. A Baptist pastor from nearby Bramhall who had occasionally preached at the chapel, offered his assistance. He shared our concern for Wilmslow and knew that four of us met to pray. He sensed God's leading and considered with us the possibility of a new venture there. God showed us in prayer that his new work was to include both the communities of Wilmslow and Alderley Edge. We placed the whole matter before him but we were still not sure whether this was the right place, or time, and we needed to know for certain.

The following Sunday I went along to the service at the chapel, asking God to show me somehow if this was his will. After some hymns and prayers, the visiting preacher got up to speak. 'And Jesus himself drew near and went with them' was his text. I needed no further confirmation. I didn't really hear the rest of the sermon. God's peace pervaded me and tears of thankfulness welled up. This was God's place for us – amazingly located right in the centre of the two communities.

We had been in Wilmslow for just under a year. Within a month, two more Christian families were led by the Lord to join us. God had formed a new praying nucleus. A lady was saved. A Sunday morning family service was introduced and later, a Sunday School. After an absence of ten years, the breaking of bread was reinstated as a central part of worship.

Jesus had more in store for us. He wanted to deal with problems that had been inherent in that church for years. He also desired to increase our faith through prayer. God's word says, 'If you believe, you will receive whatever you ask for in prayer' (Matthew 21.22). This belief is an essential ingredient of prayer. 'Without faith it is impossible to please God' (Hebrews 11.6). Together our faith was built up in the fellowship at Brook Lane as we began to claim the promises of God. One incident particularly challenged us as a church.

About a year after we had made the decision to support the

Lord's work at Brook Lane Chapel, a crisis radically affected the church: the infamous structural dry rot! Much of the chapel building was in a dangerous condition and it became clear that the structure was rapidly decaying. There then ensued a spiritual battle: had we faith in God's purposes for this place or not? By then, the church had grown to about two dozen, but by no stretch of the imagination could we provide the money to cover the repairs, let alone the improvements that were necessary to bring the building to a reasonable condition.

At a hastily convened meeting of all those connected with the chapel there was much discussion. Some were of the opinion that the building should be pulled down, as it was possible that the council could soon serve the church with a dangerous structures order. Appalled at the amount of money involved, they didn't want to be held responsible. We organised another meeting for prayer for those who seriously wanted to seek the Lord's will in this matter. Many wrestled with God that evening. It was not just the dry rot in the church fabric that was the problem – it was also the rot in our lives: unbelief, pride, our lack of love for one another and a failure to use the authority vested in us through Jesus to do God's will and to resist Satan. God required us to put away sin and to depend on the Lord Jesus Christ. He wanted to unite us in the belief that 'What is impossible with me is possible with God' (Luke 18.27).

We took a step of faith and went ahead with the repairs, believing that God would supply all the needs of the church. We were convinced that God would do this in a miraculous way without an organised appeal or sales of work which would divert our time and effort.

Praise his Name! Not only did God see to it that all the bills were paid, but we were also able to make the necessary improvements to the building! God was not just working on the financial scene – there was a noticeable deepening of fellowship, love and understanding amongst us. The prayer life of the church was invigorated as we saw daily answers to our prayers. We began to experience the effectiveness of fervent prayer. In James 5.16 it tells us that 'The effectual fervent prayer of a righteous man availeth much' (AV). We saw the need to confess our sins and become clothed in the righteousness of Jesus before we could effectively intercede for others. The church began to grow both numerically and spiritually as people were saved.

Another event was to have a marked influence on our prayer life as a family. This also involved the whole church fellowship as they prayed with us and for us and so through it we experienced the love and care of God's people. But I must leave Verena to tell the story, as it concerns the birth of our son Philip.

'Therefore, brothers, since we have confidence to enter the Most Holy Place by the blood of Jesus . . . let us draw near to God' (Hebrews 10.19,22). Jesus died on the cross so that we could have a right relationship with God. It is only through Jesus that we can enter God's presence with confidence and ask for those things which concern us, believing that we receive what we ask for. It was this confidence that we began to experience as we learned to approach God boldly and claim his promises, even when things seemed to be going drastically wrong.

I was lying in my hospital bed listening to the heartbeat of the baby inside me. I had a disc strapped to my tummy over the place where the baby's heart was located and this was wired up to the machine beside me. The disc picked up the baby's heartbeat which was then amplified by the machine so that it was audible. A graph was being drawn at the same time giving a visible progress report on the baby's condition. Periodically one of the nursing staff would come over to see how I was getting on, take a look at the graph and check the position of the disc. I could hear other foetal heartbeats in the same room: two other ladies were strapped up in a similar fashion. The regular chug chug of their machines was quite reassuring, like a steam train going steadily along the level. But there was something quite different about the sound coming from mine. My train chugged painfully slowly to the top of a steep incline and then, once it had gained the summit, gathered speed and rushed down the other side. Then would come another incline and another slow haul. There was something terribly wrong, I thought. The sound should be steady – a regular speed – like the sound of the other babies in the ward.

I was seven months pregnant and had gone into hospital that day because of concern for the baby after an ante-natal check-up. No one seemed to know what was wrong. As I lay there I remembered how, only a few days before, a friend of ours had prayed for the safe delivery of our baby. At the time she prayed I had thought it rather early to pray like that – after all, the baby wasn't due for another two months, but now I could only marvel at the Lord's timing and the moving of the Holy Spirit as I felt confident that God would answer her prayer.

Jesus says, 'If you remain in me and my words remain in you, ask whatever you wish, and it will be given you' (John 15.7). We had prayed for this baby and knew that the Lord was going to give us another son, Philip. What we hadn't foreseen were the problems I was to encounter during the pregnancy, with an early threatened miscarriage, and now this. I couldn't do anything else but cling on to what I knew God had promised us and put my confidence in him. 'And this is the confidence that we have in him, that, if we ask anything according to his will, he heareth us: And if we know that he hear us, whatsoever we ask, we know that we have the petitions that we desired of him' (1 John 5.14–15, AV).

The baby's heartbeat was monitored every few hours over the next two days. Saturday was very busy with a number of emergency deliveries, including a few Caesarian sections, so there was plenty to occupy the hospital staff. In the meantime, I began to feel more uncomfortable and now could only lie on one side although my 'lump' was still quite small. The monitoring machine delivered its unsympathetic message every few hours. It sounded as though the baby was having a hard time of it, his heartbeat becoming more and more erratic. Eventually I turned the sound down, unable to bear it any longer. That evening, for the first time, I began to get worried. 'Lord, something's got to be done soon,' I prayed, 'things are getting fairly desperate – the baby is having a terrible time. Lord, you promised us this baby so I know he's going to be all right. Help me to trust you in this situation, even though it isn't looking too good.' Two sentences from Philippians 4 came into my mind: 'Do not be anxious about anything, but in everything by prayer and petition, with thanksgiving, present your requests to God. And the peace of God, which transcends all understanding will guard your hearts and your minds in Christ Jesus' (vv. 6–7). Immediately I knew this peace in my heart and I fell into an untroubled sleep – so much so, that the doctor who had come specifically to see me that night, did not like to disturb me.

The next morning I woke up ravenously hungry, wondering what was for breakfast. It came shortly: cereal, bacon, tomatoes, fried bread and toast, all of which I ate heartily along with two cups of tea. At ten-thirty the doctor came back to see me and presented the bombshell – he wanted to operate at twelve noon! I thought ruefully of the huge breakfast I had just eaten. I hadn't expected my prayer of the previous evening to be answered quite so soon! A general anaesthetic on top of all that food! But the doctors didn't want to delay any longer. I prayed briefly and left the situation with the Lord, hoping that the anaesthetist knew his stuff – in fact, after the operation I had no ill effects apart from a sore throat!

I had some difficulty getting hold of Henry. I knew he would already be at church and would have enough to do looking after our three other children. The hospital staff encouraged me to try and locate him so I telephoned a friend living in Brook Lane near the chapel. He dropped everything and raced down to the church where the service was still in progress. I heard afterwards that all proceedings were abandoned and the fellowship started praying for me and the baby. Henry was able to leave the children to the care of the fellowship. In his haste he also left a wet nappy in the church hall! He arrived just in time to accompany me down to the theatre.

Philip was born safe and sound soon afterwards while the church was still in prayer. The doctors discovered that the umbilical cord was wrapped twice round his neck and that there was a large blood clot where the cord joined the placenta. It was doubtful whether the baby would have lived much longer. He weighed in at 3lb 13oz, a sturdy weight for a two-month premature baby and, although he had to stay in the special care unit in hospital for a month, there was nothing wrong with him at all. Now, nearly two years later, he is a happy, healthy child and we still regard him as our miracle baby. 'The Lord is faithful to all his promises and loving towards all he has made' (Psalm 145.13).

Throughout our Christian walk we have drawn great encouragement from the prayer support of God's people and we are still learning more about the power of prayer. We have found a confidence that comes from the knowledge of being in God's will. We can trust him for the smallest detail of our lives because we know he loves and cares for us.

We have mentioned just some of the experiences that we've had on our Emmaus Road with Jesus. God has shown us that if we walk humbly before him in total obedience, putting our faith expectantly in his word, we will develop the kind of prayer life we should have. Confident that we will receive God's answers, we can joyfully anticipate the next phase of the journey. Praise the Lord for the ever closer relationship God intends for us to enjoy through a deeper prayer life with the Lord Jesus Christ!

Julie Halsey

Prayer: Under Pressure

Trained as a secretary at Loughborough Technical College. My first full time job was in a Leicester advertising agency. From there I moved to London to join the staff on *Buzz*, looking after the advertising and some editorial work. It was whilst working there I met Noël, and we got married in 1976. I then went back to doing secretarial work, first in computers, then insurance. I did some market research part-time while we were starting our own business. We are now living in Milton Keynes and are members of Stony Stratford Baptist Church. We also help in the running of an outreach church on one of the city's grid squares. At the moment I am a housewife and mother.

It's six-thirty in the morning and a muttering voice is heard from the next bedroom. The voice is gradually getting louder and I realise the Teddy Bears are getting a strong lecture about something. My mind is sleepy and unco-operative. 'Good morning, God.' Crash! The bedroom door handle slams against the wall; a thudding of feet comes across the landing and the two-year-old bursts in like a cowboy through a saloon door.

'Mummy . . . Teddy.' One bear is plonked on to my head, and the softer one gets wedged in beside me. A pair of pink pyjamas scramble over the duvet: 'Cuddle, Mummy.' God has already been relegated to second in the queue for my attention. Any attempts now to have a sensible conversation with my Lord and Saviour are doomed to interruption. I hear: 'Mummy, tea please', followed by, 'Nappy wet – off' while the bouncing up and down of an energetic toddler throws my body into perpetual motion.

'Please, Lord, help me get through today,' is all I manage as I charge after Rowena, now rapidly heading for baby Simeon's cot. 'No, Rowena, baby boy's not awake – his eyes are closed. Come on, let's have you in the bath.'

Last thing at night and first thing in the morning are two times we must pray. This is what I believe, and my Christian reading has confirmed it. One writer's words have been a constant reminder to me:

'Your last thoughts as you fall asleep should be of God, His goodness and His love . . . when you give your mind spiritual thoughts to dwell on, they will permeate your being during the night and provide the best start to the day. On waking, thank Him for a good night's sleep. Then thank

Him for a new day. Commit things to Him for His control.'

But where does that leave me? Yes, I know the truth of what is said, and am almost ridden with guilt by my neglect on some mornings to pray. My start to the day is far from being so serene and well-organised; my brain shifts into gear more readily after a cup of tea than anything more spiritual, and, horror of horrors, on the occasions when I start contemplating the Lord my concentration wanders off the greatness of God to some more mundane subject like, 'Will the nappies dry outside today?'

If I could get myself disciplined and sufficiently motivated, no doubt I'd be rivalling the great saints kneeling devotedly by their beds at five o'clock in the morning. But rather than rising to the challenge of such glowing examples of faith I am discouraged – it is something way out of my own experience. For me, five in the morning doesn't exist.

Later in the day my problem is the 'devotion' bit – spending time praying and doing nothing else, and Martin Luther's words haunt me in the hurry of the day: 'I have so much to do that I shall spend the first three hours daily in prayer.'

As soon as the children are awake there is very little time for concentrating on anything – and that includes prayer. My brain is overloaded with trying not to boil the milk over, wondering what to have for dinner and thinking about half a dozen other things that cannot wait. So I compromise. I just try to obey the command to 'pray at all times' and achieve 'praying sometimes' – maybe talking to God while doing the washing-up – and perhaps I manage a bit of singing prayer like 'In my life, Lord, be glorified, Oh, be glorified . . . .' But I know I'm not really giving God much of a chance to transform me into the person he wants me to be. Real prayer is life-changing as God gently and graciously shows how he sees things and instils a desire for his will. Not to pray is to deny God free access to make me more like him. What a battle!

There are times during the day when a response to God is

provoked by a situation and prayer wells up quite naturally. For me one of these times is early morning when the baby wakes up. As I bend over his cot to turn him over he gives one of his wide-mouthed, toothless smiles and I feel such gratitude to God welling up inside me that I grin back at my baby boy thinking, 'Thank you, Father, for your wonderful gift.' Not only does that glorify God, but it makes me happy knowing that God is listening and understands completely. It is also an emotional safety-valve for me to share what I feel with God.

Sometimes prayer takes precedence over everything else – like the evening my husband was on his way out to an important meeting where people would be hearing the gospel. He shouted 'Goodnight' at me through the bathroom door, and, 'Will you remember to pray for the evening?'

'Let's pray before you go,' I shouted back, knowing it would be far safer to pray there and then than to rely on my imcompetent memory. He squeezed through the bathroom door, carefully negotiating baby boy on his changing mat on the floor. We put our arms round each other and committed the evening to God's protection, asking him to be present in that meeting. Rowena stopped washing herself with her sponge and looked interested. You could see her mind working: 'Mummy and Daddy having a cuddle, and they're ignoring me.' A quick goodnight kiss for them both and off he went, but at least we had prayed.

As husband and wife we have always tried to pray together at night; that is the time when we can usually guarantee to be together, free from interruption, though of course, it has its disadvantages in that occasionally we are both so tired that we fall asleep without doing our Bible reading and praying, especially if we're late to bed. We pray about the events of the day, special plans for the future, our basic needs, people we've been in contact with, and together bring our family before the Lord for his blessing.

Involvement in running a Christian business has meant that we have had to rely heavily on God to provide, not just for us, but also for the business to be kept viable. Time after time we have had to ask God at what has seemed to us like the eleventh hour, to find that in the nick of time he steps in to answer. It is a relief to us that we can take cares and concerns to him in prayer, and leave the burden of our problems with him.

There have been difficult times when we have known God's answers to prayer in a different way from the way we'd expected him to answer. We'd been praying for business premises for almost a year and no office or warehouse space was forthcoming. The situation was getting quite desperate. We had a small end of terrace house in Kent. Noël was using the box room as his office; I was using the dining table for the typewriter and moving everything when it was time to eat. Every available inch of the bedroom floors was carpeted with boxes of greeting cards, and the single garage was stacked to the ceiling. We took the problem to the Lord: 'God, you know we can't carry on like this.'

Noël felt that God was telling us to move to Milton Keynes. It wasn't quite the answer we had expected, our idea for premises had been something local, but God performed the impossible to get us to move where he wanted us to be. Amazingly, he provided a small business unit in Milton Keynes. When we heard about them all the small units had been taken, but a cancellation came up, which we took.

We found a house just a few minutes' drive from the new business premises; it was just perfect, but was £3,000 more than we could afford. Again we had to trust God. The builders were prepared to drop the price by exactly that amount, but only if we exchanged contracts within six weeks. With our own house to sell it was virtually impossible. We called an estate agent for a valuation and asked him what the chances were of a quick sale. 'Houses aren't selling at the moment,' he said, 'it's the wrong time. Of course, we'll do our best.' We asked if he minded us trying to sell the house privately. That didn't matter at all;

he was convinced it wouldn't sell in a hurry. But we committed it to the Lord and placed a small advert in the local weekly paper. By the end of the week we'd had five sets of people to view and three couples wanted to buy. God had again answered prayer.

The final hurdle to cross was getting a mortgage in six weeks. We tried through a broker, and after three weeks had elapsed he announced that he was unable to secure us a mortgage. We went to our bank – they took what seemed like ages and I was beginning to feel uneasy. After sending a surveyor to look at the proposed property, the bank turned down our request for a mortgage. By this time we were both beginning to question if we had really discerned the Lord's will correctly. Our purchasers were pushing us, and I didn't think it would inspire them with confidence if we gave them the facts: 'We're trusting God to secure us a mortgage.'

With only a week to go before the contracts were due to be exchanged we approached our building society. 'D' day loomed up, and no confirmation came through. The temptation to stop trusting God and panic was very strong, and every time I considered the human impossibility of the situation I felt practically sick with worry. It was not the eleventh hour: by English lawyers' standards it had passed midnight. We still trusted in God. That trust was not misplaced. On the very day we were due to exchange contracts the building society agreed to advance us the money we needed. In the normal way, written confirmation – the usual legal requirement – could have taken up to another week; a week that we did not have. Instead, the building society offered to phone the solicitor with verbal confirmation of the offer, enabling him to proceed with the exchange of contracts. And so it went through. Our solicitor was genuinely amazed, and admitted to Noël, 'In all my years of conveyancing, I have never known a building society to be so helpful.' God had kept us waiting beyond what we thought was the last moment, but when he revealed his greatness to us in answered prayer, we realised that his timing had been no less than perfect.

The contracts went through without a hitch as the purchasers of our house had already sold theirs to a first time buyer; we got the new house at the dropped price and what's more, it had cost just £7.50 to sell our old one. God had answered so very practically. Looking back, we could see that everything had been slotted into place by him, but when we were going through it, our faith and trust in the Lord to supply the answers we needed before it was too late was severely tested.

To be able to come before God, regardless of the time or the place, and know that he always hears is a privilege. It is marvellous when I ask God for something specific in a particular immediate situation and he answers straight away. Often it is only something little. I am in the car and needing a parking space and there are none, so in desperation I pray, 'Father God, please supply a parking space' – and immediately a car draws out from a spot right under my nose. So it happens once and I label it as coincidence, twice and I think I'm fortunate, and the third time I just have to acknowledge that it's God's direct answer to my prayer. Then I have to thank him for the way he shows his love, and I am forced to remember what a great, powerful God we really have.

Some of the most dynamic and exciting times of prayer that I can remember have been shared with other Christians. United prayer has a special blessing from God: 'Where two or three are gathered together in my name, there am I in the midst of them' (Matthew 18.20). I remember an evening fellowship on a Sunday after church. Several of us arrived together at the house where the meeting was already in progress. The front door was unlocked and as I entered the hall I felt the presence of God. It was so powerful that I fully expected to see Jesus standing in the lounge where the others were praying. That room was filled with the sense of the Lord being there. We were praying for about two hours, waiting on the Lord and it was exhilarating. The time passed so rapidly that it seemed just like a few minutes and I understood the meaning of the words, 'They that wait upon the Lord shall renew their strength.' Even the air seemed to smell of God, the light seemed to be God's brightness, and the warmth a temperature controlled by him, just perfectly comfortable. It was the first time I had experienced God in that sort of way. Occasionally since I have felt the closeness of the Lord while praying, but never as vividly as then.

God's powerful answer to prayer through healing is one of the most amazing things I have witnessed and been able to prove in my own life. I had heard people tell of healings, but although not doubting the ability of God to perform a modern-day miracle, somehow my mind just stumbled at the idea of the supernatural power of God being revealed so physically. One Sunday I really had to marvel at God's power to heal. I'd hurt my back and any position was uncomfortable. Sitting was quite painful and during a time of prayer I was asked if I wanted prayer for my back. Several people prayed and then the wife of one of the church deacons put her arms around me, placing her hands on my aching back. 'Where does it hurt?' she asked, and laying her hand on the sore spot, prayed for the Lord's healing. As she prayed a warmth seemed to come from her hands and flow into the pain, dispersing it and relaxing the tired muscles. God had taken away the pain, healing the trouble instantly. At first I couldn't bring myself to say anything, hardly daring to believe that the Lord had worked a miracle, yet I could sit comfortably without cushions and stand normally – it must be an answer to prayer. After making absolutely sure that I was not imagining that the pain had been taken away, I told the group and everyone was thrilled.

There have been a few times when prayer has brought me into a new dimension, where God's presence is so vital and real that my mind no longer has to strain to concentrate, when the Holy Spirit has prompted in such a miraculous way that God has been superbly easy to talk to. He has been there and communicating to me, and although there may be others in the room it has been essentially a personal experience. Prayer has been made easy: it's like being lifted up by the hands of God into a position so close to him that no effort is required on my behalf. Then God shows me a little of his glory and greatness, lets me taste his gentleness and love for me, shows his mercy and grace and pours out forgiveness, making me clean before him and renewing and refreshing me. Confronted by God in that sort of way, prayer ceases to be the making of requests, the recitation of a list of needs, and changes into praise prompted by the Holy Spirit, into gratitude, adoration of God's holiness and confession of my own sinfulness. Only then follows a fulfilled enjoyment of God, and real delight in his presence. Unfortunately, times like this are few and far between. More often, I feel God showing me the dearth in my prayer life.

There are many times when I have found prayer quite difficult. On those occasions having a structure in praying has been helpful. To actually get started is hard, and although the Holy Spirit is the One who prompts prayer, there is also quite a lot of room for self-discipline. Just getting into a room which is quiet and closing the door is the effort I have to make in simple obedience to God. 'When you pray, go into your room, close the door and pray to your Father, who is unseen' (Matthew 6.6). Having got that far what I have found helpful is to read a passage of Scripture, maybe a Psalm, and use that to put me in the right frame of mind to pray, or to use daily reading notes (which don't always get done daily) as a sort of spring-board from which to start. Often by having some stimulation from a devotional reading it is easier to focus my mind on God.

I have tried some practical aids to prayer, like following a pattern such as the Lord's Prayer, and taking that line by line, expanding on each thought. At other times I concentrate on beginning by praising and thanking God for what he has done. Even if I can't find anything to thank him for I can always thank him for Jesus. Then I bring myself to him in confession and claim his promise that 'If we confess our sins, he is faithful and just and will forgive us our sins and purify us from all unrighteousness' (1 John 1.9). Then I pray for other people or things which I feel the Lord is laying on my heart. Sometimes there will be a situation of which I have only limited knowledge and having prayed as intelligently as possible with the information available, then I am grateful to God for the gift of tongues to describe more fully and deeply the things my mind cannot adequately express. 'Likewise the Spirit helps us in our weakness; for we do not know how to pray as we ought, but the Spirit himself intercedes for us with sighs too deep for words' (Romans 8.26, RSV). Finally, I listen to God for his comments on the situations I've brought to him. So often it's easy to do all the talking and not give God an opportunity to speak and show me his perspective on things.

In some respects I find it much easier to pray with someone else than on my own. Their presence and concentration helps me and is encouraging. One day I made up my mind that I needed someone with whom I could honestly share and openly pray, and since then God has provided close Christian friends with the same desire to pray with me on a regular basis.

Whilst going through College I explained to the Lord that I felt very alone as a Christian. Straight away I met Barbara who was also a Christian. Although we were very different we got on tremendously well, and started meeting once a week to do some Bible study together and to pray about the things we came up against in College life: the people we knew, their need for God and our own problems. God taught me a lot during our time together and we both grew in our knowledge and love for him.

Later, when I was at work and, as far as I know, the only Christian there, the Lord convinced another girl, Lizzie, who had always been a close friend at my home church, that he wanted us to pray together. The time we spent together praying was so unlike formal church prayer times: the

Lord's presence was real and every time we met God was saying something very directly to us. We felt he was calling us both individually into full-time work for him. It was as if the Lord was with us in the room and gently asking us to obey him as he showed us where he wanted us to go. We knew that he would not force us against our wills, but had showed us the direction and it was up to us whether we were willing to obey. It was a tussle for us to put God first but Lizzie went to Bible College, and I into full-time Christian work. In being obedient to what he asked me to do I found that he had already prepared the road ahead of me and made his provision for my needs. One of the good things that stemmed from being in the 'right' place was meeting my husband!

In many areas of prayer I am only a learner and have had little experience. One such area is spiritual warfare: taking authority over the power of the enemy. We are told that the battle which we are called to fight is 'not against flesh and blood, but against the principalities, against the powers, against the world rulers of this present darkness, against the spiritual hosts of wickedness in the heavenly places' (Ephesians 6.12, RSV). In this battle it is the power that there is in prayer which will gain the victory, as by faith we claim the promises of God. Perhaps, along with many other Christians, when pushed into a corner by the devil I will take authority over him, but am reluctant to go on the offensive unless provoked.

I have also much to learn in the area of asking God to heal through prayer and the laying on of hands. There are amazing verses of Scripture that declare God's willingness to answer prayer: 'If you abide in me, and my words abide in you, ask whatever you will, and it shall be done for you' (John 15.7, RSV).

The conclusion I am forced to draw is that I am not 'abiding'; not maintaining unbroken fellowship with God by walking in the Spirit and keeping the conditions he has set. A victorious prayer life stems from leading a holy life, and it's not easy.

In the area of 'praying at all times in the Spirit' (Ephesians 6.18) well, I haven't got anywhere near that. The things written about here are the times when I have prayed, and so it perhaps gives a very unbalanced picture of how my time is really spent. Proportionately, praying takes a very small amount of time in relation to the hours spent involved in other things. And yet when I look back and see God's answers to prayer it makes me wonder what I would be seeing had I prayed more fervently and with greater dedication. I am challenged by my lack of prayer and realise that I'm on the bottom rung of the ladder. Along with the disciples I have to say, 'Lord, teach me to pray.'

Jim Binney

Overcoming Failure in Prayer

Jim Binney was born at Greenford, Middlesex. He came to faith in Christ in his mid-teens. While employed by a large civil-engineering company he was called to full-time ministry. After four years training at Spurgeon's College he began his first pastorate at Bewdley, Worcestershire. This church grew rapidly under his leadership.

While at Bewdley he met the late Pastor W. H. T. Richards of Slough Gospel Tabernacle. This led to his joining the pastoral team at Slough as an itinerant preacher. Following the death of Bill Richards he went to Newbridge, Gwent to become pastor of the Assemblies of God Church.

Sensing the call of God back into the Baptist denomination he became pastor of Mitcham Lane, Streatham in 1977. Following an exciting period of growth in the church, the pastorate ended in 1980 in the circumstances described in this chapter.

Jim then spent a period of two years in insurance before becoming pastor of Teddington Baptist Church, where he is at present.

He and his wife Pam have two children, Caroline and David. Jim is a keen sportsman. He has played cricket and football to good club standard.

We have been rightly told that 'prayer is the Christian's vital breath'! If this is the case, why is it that we Christians seem to pray so little? A recent survey produced the startling figures that the average Christian spends approximately sixty seconds a day in prayer! As you would expect, the clergy come out somewhat better. The average clergyman spends approximately ninety seconds a day in prayer!

Is it not true to say that prayer is bound to be a battle ground? If prayer really is vital to the Christian life and walk will Satan not do all he can to defeat us in this realm? Did Jesus deliberately go into the desert, following his baptism, to confront Satan (Luke 4.1ff) or was he not put under Satanic attack because he went there alone to pray and wait on God his Father in prayer regarding his imminent public ministry (see Luke 5.16)? Is Paul's powerful call to prayer in Ephesians 6.18–20 really separate from all that he has to say earlier in the chapter about spiritual warfare? No, Satan is bound to attack us here. We should not be surprised if maintaining a vibrant prayer life – individually, in the family, corporately in the church – is a battle. I believe that the majority of Christians find this. If we had the opportunity to ask the Lord Jesus for one thing I suspect most of us would echo the first disciples' request, 'Lord teach us to pray' (Luke 11.1).

This is not to say that we cannot overcome failure. We can. But we can only do it by facing up to our failures honestly, rather than by pretending that we are 'mighty in prayer' if we are not. Also we have to be determined that by the grace of God we will win through into the place of victory in this spiritual warfare.

I have found some things particularly helpful for overcoming failure in prayer.

Honesty

If we are to overcome failure in prayer we must be absolutely honest – with ourselves, with others, and above all, with God! We must, however, be honest without being morbid or negative as is the tendency of some. Spurgeon, in his *Lectures to my Students*, tells of one poor man in a prayer meeting so overtaken by the thought that both he and his whole family were but 'dust' in God's sight that his sad prayer was, 'O Lord, save Thy dust, and Thy dust's dust, and Thy dust's dust's dust'! A defeatist attitude reveals very little understanding of the true nature of God, a God whose most prominent characteristic is love (1 John 4.16); a God who loves us with a love which is beyond comprehension and who demonstrated that love by sending his Son to die for us (Romans 5.5–11); a God who sent Jesus to seek and to save the lost (Luke 19.10). It is because our God is such a God that we can, at any time in any condition, boldly approach him (Hebrews 4.14–16) – even if it is to ask for forgiveness and restoration! We must begin by being honest with ourselves about ourselves! The next best thing to knowing that you are right is knowing that you are wrong! If you know that something is wrong you can do something about it. If something is wrong and you don't know it (or won't admit it) then nothing can be done about it!

This honesty with ourselves must become honesty before God, however, if any change is to take place. In reality God knows all about us anyway (Psalm 139) and it is foolish to hide from him. In one of my former pastorates there was a family who had a little girl of about three years of age. Whenever anyone called whom she did not know well she would put her hands up in front of her eyes. Because she could not see them she thought they could not see her! God knows all there is to know about us, but he wants to hear from our lips our confession of failure and need! To be honest with God can be a very humbling experience. Read David's great confession of failure before God in Psalm 51! We not only read it, we feel it! And yet is not this the very secret of forgiveness and restoration and renewal? How wonderful are the words of 1 John 1.9 – 'If we confess our sins, he is faithful and just, and will forgive our sins and cleanse us from all unrighteousness' (RSV). As Phillips Brooks once said, 'You must learn, you must let God teach you, that the only way to get rid of your past is to get a future out of it. God will waste nothing. There are worse things, in God's sight, than failure. Hyprocrisy is one. Grovelling in the gutter wishing that we had not fallen over, instead of getting up and going to God for cleansing and restoration, is another.'

Renewal, not least in the area of prayer, came for many of us when we began to be honest with ourselves about ourselves before God. In 1965, when I entered Spurgeon's College to train for the Baptist ministry, I was (like many theological students) rather full of myself! Prior to entering college I had done reasonably well academically and in industry. I was well thought of in my home church. I had been youth leader and had even been elected to the Diaconate just after my twenty-first birthday. I had a growing reputation as an 'up and coming young preacher' and my attitude was 'OK, God, you can sit back now, Jim Binney's arrived!'

Needless to say, my first two years at college were somewhat of a disaster in many ways. I struggled academically and found the whole thing tough going, not least spiritually. By the beginning of my third year at Spurgeon's I was pretty much at the end of myself, although I was still not prepared to admit it. Everything came to a head when I was summoned home from college urgently because my father was dying of cancer and only had three weeks to live. At the time I was the only 'committed' Christian in the family and yet I found it impossible to talk to my father about Christ, even though we both knew he was dying. In fact I found the whole situation impossible to cope with, and if it hadn't been for my mother I would have completely fallen apart. Shortly before he died my father, who was an ex-army man of the old school and a real fighter, fell back on his pillow one day and simply said, 'I'm finished!'

Those words stayed with me for weeks afterwards. Through them God spoke to me. Here was my father dying of cancer (which in my mind I somehow associated with sin) crying out, 'I'm finished!' In my mind this contrasted with the words of Jesus on the cross, as he triumphed over Satan, sin and death: 'It is finished!' (John 19.30). One the cry of defeat, the other the cry of victory! I found myself praying, 'Lord why is it, if Jesus won such a victory, that I am so defeated by self, by my besetting sins, by my powerlessness?' My problem was compounded by the fact that, despite my deep dissatisfaction with my own spiritual condition, I had experienced enough of the Lord in my life since my conversion to know that God was real and that the lack in my life was in me and not in him. There was only one way to go and that was forward.

I returned to college, chastened and broken in spirit, and began to pray as I had never prayed before. The burden of my prayer was for personal revival. I did not know what that entailed, I did not dictate to the Lord how it should come. I simply asked God to meet with me. For the best part of two months I prayed. I prayed early in the morning, I prayed late into the night. I prayed during the day. This was unlike the former me who talked of prayer rather than did it! I seemed under a God-given compulsion to pray. I had a hunger and thirst for God to bring me into a new place in himself. It was a time of great heart-searching when I seemed to learn so much about myself simply by waiting on the Lord. In a wonderful way I found others in college to pray with who felt as I did. I did not realise it but there were, at that time, ones and twos all over college feeling exactly as I did. Gradually we came into contact with one another, and often we would meet together in the college chapel or in one another's rooms, late in the evening to pray. During this two-month period my life gradually changed as God taught me some deep lessons, and I was prepared to face up to some 'home truths' about myself. Alongside my compulsion to pray came a new compulsion to read the Bible. I searched the Scriptures for an answer to my need. I was not looking for a 'charismatic experience' or any experience for that matter. I was looking for personal revival – however the Lord sought to send it.

One Monday evening towards the end of October 1968, whilst praying with some others in the college chapel, God answered my prayer. It is difficult to put into exact words what happened that night – to put it simply I would say that the Holy Spirit fell upon me and filled me in a way I had never experienced before. Some eight years before I had had a very real conversion experience. I knew an assurance of my salvation in personal experience. But this was altogether greater – a sense of deep cleansing from sin and failure as the Spirit washed over me, followed by a tremendous sense of empowering as the Spirit flowed through me, and then an overwhelming sense of joy, and release (so much so that I began to both laugh and cry at the same time) as the Spirit filled me. I later found my own experience perfectly summarised in an account by Samuel Chadwick of his own experience of seeking God for personal revival – 'Twelve of us began to pray in a band and the answer came . . . God led us to Pentecost. The key to all my life is in that experience. It awakened my mind as well as cleansed my heart. It gave me a new joy and a new power, a new love and a new compassion. It gave me a new Bible and a new message. Above all else it gave me a new intimacy in the communion and ministry of prayer; it taught me to pray in the Spirit' (*The Path of Prayer*).

Praying in the Spirit

I remember very little of that night after this experience. My friends, with whom I had been praying, described me as having been 'drunk with the Spirit'. Two of them took me back to my room where all I can remember is seeming to spend the night in heaven – 'lost in wonder, love and praise'. At some point I must have drifted into sleep because I remember waking early the next morning knowing that things were different – radically so. This was especially true in the realm of prayer. I found myself praying in a totally new way. To begin with, there was a new sense of praise and thankfulness to God in my praying. Then there was a new sensitivity to the voice of God, almost like a partially deaf man regaining his full hearing. There was also a new concern for others. Whereas much of my prayer had previously been centred on myself I found myself that first morning pouring out my heart to God for various other people. Some were people I had never seriously prayed for before and yet somehow I knew it was right to pray for them.

Whilst praying for two people in particular I felt more deeply moved to pray than ever before and found myself interceding for them with tears running down my cheeks. Now I was not really the sort to cry like that. I was six feet three inches tall, thirteen stone in weight, and would have previously considered such behaviour in a man rather 'over the top' emotionally. For perhaps the first time I felt I was really 'getting through' in prayer for people. At the same time I became aware that I was praying in 'another language' foreign to my own. I had not sought 'the gift of tongues', and I had not even been aware that I was 'speaking in tongues', and had been for several minutes, until that moment.

For several weeks after this prayer was a thrilling adventure. I learnt so much about really praising and thanking God in the secret place and about just waiting on the Lord (Isaiah 40.31, AV). During this period I felt the Lord directing me to the book of Exodus, which I studied prayerfully day by day, learning so much from the parallel between Israel's escape from the bondage of Egypt to the blessings of the promised land and my own deliverance from the bondage of sin into the liberty of God. I learnt so much about intercession, too, during this time – not always praying in tongues, by the way, although I did find the gift wonderful when it came to praying for those for whom I felt burdened yet about whom I didn't know enough to enter really prayerfully into their situation. Perhaps my whole experience during this time, and the important lesson learned from it, is best summarised in the words of J. Stuart Holden – 'How many Christians there are who cannot pray, and who seek by effort, resolve, joining prayer circles etc. to cultivate in themselves the "holy art of intercession" and all to no purpose. Here for them and for all is the only secret of a real prayer life – "Be filled with the Spirit" who is the Spirit of grace and supplication.'

Of course it was not possible, nor was it right, I believe, to continue to live at such a height of intensity. There was so much that I had to learn over the months and years that followed about what it really meant to be daily 'filled with the Spirit' (Ephesians 5.18) – about walking in the Spirit without grieving or quenching the Spirit; about repentance when I did fail; about forgiving myself as well as accepting God's forgiveness when I confessed my sin; about putting things right with others as well as God; about living the Christ-centred life, and not a Holy Spirit-centred life (see John 16.13–15); about the meaning of true discipleship; about 'spiritual warfare'. But in it all I did discover that the God of the mountain top was also the God of the valley.

Praying Together

We often remind ourselves of the lovely promise of Jesus that 'Where two or three come together in my name, there am I with them' (Matthew 18.20). I have heard this particular verse used in many contexts and applied to various situations but I have rarely heard it applied in the context in which it appears in the Bible, which seems to me to be the context of corporate prayer. The preceding two verses speak of binding and loosing, and of agreeing together prayerfully. It seems that here Jesus is promising us his special presence in the place of corporate prayer. This can range from, say, a married couple praying together, through a small prayer 'cell', to a church prayer meeting. Over the years I have always sought to encourage greater corporate prayer in the churches I have been privileged to serve.

When I entered the ministry in 1969, my first pastorate was Bewdley Baptist Church, Worcestershire. My wife, Pam, and I were newly married. From the beginning we gave ourselves to prayer for the church, knowing that if there was to be blessing and growth God had to give it and prayer was his method. It was here that we learned some deep lessons, which have stood us in good stead over the years. We learned about the power of prayer, about how God meets us as together we seek his face for the way forward, and about his power working through prayer as we intercede for an area and its people. Not only did Pam and I pray together, but we often met with another couple in the church, Robert and Anne Wildgoose, who shared our concern and vision. We would meet together for prayer several evenings each week, usually meeting about ten in the evening (the work still had to be done) and sometimes praying until two or three o'clock in the morning. Looking back on it, I wonder how we managed to keep it up. We were younger then, I suppose, but also we did know a quite remarkable sense of the Lord's presence.

Early on, God gave us a vision of a stone being thrown into a pond and the ripples going out. To us this was a prophetic picture of what he planned to do in Bewdley and in the area. Over the next few years we saw a lovely movement of God in the church, with a large number of people being converted, baptised and filled with the Spirit. We also saw some quite remarkable healings – a young child suffering from partial deafness and ear ache so severe that she would sit and bang her head on the floor to try and relieve the pain; a young married woman told she would never have children; a young man partially blind, an older lady who had suffered with angina for many years, and many others, each a story in itself. Our second child, David (we also have an older daughter, Caroline) was born with a serious heart condition. So much was wrong with him that the doctors told us that it was impossible for him to live. His condition was deemed so serious that no operation was possible. All we could do was pray. The whole fellowship prayed, and so did many Christian friends throughout the country. A few days later the hospital sent for us to tell us that there was better news – a 'spontaneous correction' had taken place and although he still had a heart defect he was out of danger. David is now eleven and although he still has an annual check-up, the medical people are very happy with his progress and to all appearances he is just a normal boy who loves football, fun and getting into mischief.

During this time in Bewdley the spirit of prayer grew in the church. When we first went there we had no regular midweek meeting for prayer and Bible study. Eventually I managed to persuade the church to fit in some time at eight-thirty on a Thursday evening after choir practice. I vividly remember one lady saying she would come as long as we finished by nine o'clock and I took her home in the car afterwards! How different this beginning was to the church prayer meeting we held regularly each week on Monday evenings some eighteen months or so afterwards. We held it because the people wanted it, not because the pastor insisted on it. We met on Thursdays to study God's word, and on Mondays to pray. Of course we had to learn to pray together. Those first Thursday meetings contained 'prayer times' (we had to fit Bible study in as well) very much in 'old style'. People would come to a prayer meeting and *not* pray out loud. Some of those who did would pray 'round the world'. We did tend to 'dot around' all over the place in prayer. We weren't very good at listening to God, either. But at least we prayed. Gradually we learned to wait on God, to know the mind of Christ in our praying, realising that the secret of effective prayer is to ask God to do that which he wants to do (see 1 John 5.14–15). We learned to listen to God. William Barclay says, 'We are apt to think that prayer is asking God for what we want, whereas true prayer is asking God for what he wants. We are apt to think of prayer as talking to God – as indeed it is – whereas, it is even more listening to God!' We learned to pray through an issue, and not pray 'round the world' or present God with a 'shopping list' of requests. We learned to praise God first and then to intercede. Often the whole course of a prayer meeting would change as a result of a revelation God gave us in a prayer meeting, either through a passage of scripture, or a word of prophecy, or a word of knowledge or wisdom.

To this day I am convinced that each local church needs a vital church prayer meeting. No doubt the critics can come up with various reasons why this is not so – the advent of house groups, for example, but I still believe a vital church prayer meeting is the 'power house' of the local church. Every church I have served has had one (with the exception of my present church at Teddington – and that will come). They have had them, not at my insistence, but because the people themselves saw the need and asked for one!

When I left Bewdley and became an Associate Minister at the Gospel Tabernacle, Slough, Bucks (now Slough Christian Centre) on the Christian Witness side of the work there, they already had a vital church prayer meeting. W. T. H. Richards, the senior minister and a godly man from whom I learned much, was a great believer in prayer and was certain that work was built on prayer as much as on anything else. When later, following the sudden death of W. T. H. Richards, I went to Newbridge, Gwent, as Pastor of the Assemblies of God church there, we again introduced a vital church prayer meeting into the programme and this made a major contribution to the work there. Whilst in Newbridge I remember one young woman being soundly converted in the prayer meeting, and I believe there were many who were converted because of the prayers of God's people in that prayer meeting.

When yet later I moved to Mitcham Lane Baptist Church, Streatham, London, we again soon had a church prayer meeting as part of the ongoing development and growth of the church. The value of this could be illustrated in several ways but one of the most striking occurred when as a fellowship we felt the Lord calling us to buy a house near the church to accommodate two students and their families – one a Brazilian pastor and the other a former church member of ours – who were going to train at Spurgeon's College (which was only a few miles away). A suitable property already divided into two flats became available and although we didn't have any money we made an offer of £30,000 for it, although the asking price was £39,000. The church caught the vision and the money miraculously came flooding in. The owner of the property gradually reduced her asking price to £32,000 and then refused to budge. She even had £1,000 worth of repairs done to the property to try and get more for it! As a church we felt that the Lord had set a ceiling of £30,000 – even getting this amount, all by free will gifts, was a wonder in itself, for we were not a large church – and so we went to further prayer.

One night in the prayer meeting the Lord spoke powerfully to us through his word and through prophecy about spiritual warfare and he showed us how Satan was seeking to thwart this venture. As a result the manner of our praying changed and for a further hour or two we prayed specifically for this house, binding the evil one and claiming the victory. Before that meeting closed we knew the house was ours! The next day the estate agent telephoned to say that, although he could not explain it, the house was ours for the figure we were prepared to pay. We called it 'Faith House'!

Failure . . . and Victory

We left Bewdley in 1973 feeling that we had achieved what the Lord sent us there to do and leaving the work in a much stronger position that when we had gone there. The Lord had also begun to fulfil the vision he had previously given to us of the stone in the pond and the ripples going out, for we saw many of the churches in the area – of various denominations – beginning to experience new life in Christ and in the power of his Spirit. To be honest, I had felt rather frustrated within the Baptist denomination, feeling that they were too 'stuck in a rut'. I felt very attracted towards the Pentecostal churches because they seemed to be much freer and more progressive. On reflection, I believe God wanted to teach me another deep lesson and so he allowed me to follow my own inclinations. I accepted an invitation to work with W. T. H. Richards in Slough. This was a valuable, if difficult time, as we learned to adjust. Just eighteen months later Mr Richards died unexpectedly, and we found ourselves again on the move, this time to South Wales to take on the pastorate of Newbridge Assemblies of God Church in Gwent. I do not believe that this was a mistake, although we never really settled there and within three years were back in London. The church did grow and we made some good friends but we did not really fit into the traditional Pentecostal scene. Perhaps the main reason from our side why God took us there was to learn more about ourselves. When I first began to feel very unsettled, Pam refused to allow me to do anything hastily, but rightly insisted that we prayed this right through. For six months we prayed, seeking the mind of Christ and waiting on God. The Lord showed us during this time that we had made a mistake in thinking that 'the grass was greener on the other side'. The Assemblies of God were no better or worse than the Baptist Church, or any other denomination for that matter. All were in need of renewal. He showed us that the Baptist denomination was where he wanted us, simply because it was his place for us. He still had 'much people' there, and since we had been saved in a Baptist church and brought up in it, it was our 'natural environment' where he wanted to use us. Having come to terms with all that God was saying to us as a result of waiting on him, we submitted.

Immediately everything started to happen. I had several approaches from larger Assemblies of God churches, several members of the Executive Council contacted me personally to ask me to remain within the movement, I even had invitations to South Africa and the USA. In it all I also had a phone call from Mitcham Lane Baptist Church, Streatham, London, right out of the blue asking if I would be interested in 'preaching with a view'! We had felt as we prayed that God was calling us not only back into the Baptist denomination but back to London. In 1977 I resigned from Newbridge and the Assemblies of God and we accepted an invitation to the pastorate of Mitcham Lane. We still have a high regard for the traditional Pentecostal movement and have many friends there. We learned much in our time with them but we had to be true to what God was calling us to.

From 1977 to 1980 we experienced in Streatham a greater move of God than anything we had seen previously, even more so than Bewdley. We were very happy there and the work was going well, too well. Pam and I were both working very hard – too hard – trying to cope with everything that was going on. Oftentimes there would be people 'queueing up' in our home – sitting waiting in different rooms to see me for 'counselling'. Again we did see many conversions, healings, people being delivered and set free, Christians 'filled with the Holy Spirit'. The church was growing fast.

But something was seriously wrong. I had stopped praying! Of course I prayed in the worship services. I prayed in the prayer meeting. I prayed with other people. I didn't pray much with Pam and the children – I hardly saw them, leave alone prayed with them! But I didn't spend time with God on my own! Looking back on it, it seems incredible, especially after all that I thought I had learned previously! I, of course, justified it. I was so busy 'helping others', so busy 'doing the Lord's work' that personal, private prayer got squeezed out. 'The Lord understands', I would tell myself. In some ways the church didn't help because there were always people who needed me, always things to be done, but I can't really blame them for my own foolish mistake. I was back to trying to do God's work in my own strength.

Things finally came to a head around Easter 1980 when I suddenly collapsed with a form of exhaustion – stress breakdown. I remember very little about it. It was like driving in sunshine and suddenly hitting a bank of fog. One minute everything was clear, and the next minute I was full of doubt. I doubted my salvation, my ministry, my marriage, my usefulness, you name it, I doubted it. My doctor later told me that it had been obvious for some time that I was doing too much and needed a complete rest. The counsellor I saw told me that I had fallen foul of the well known 'evangelical disease' of living for God and others to such an extent that I had neglected my wife, family and myself, with dire consequences.

My sudden 'collapse' sadly threw the whole church into confusion and the end product was that the leadership within the denomination felt that I should have a complete break from the ministry for at least a year. I am reminded of an incident concerning D. L. Moody who was once asked why he prayed every day and waited on God to be daily filled afresh with the Holy Spirit, since he had experienced a mighty 'baptism with the Spirit' previously. Moody's reply was simply, 'I leak!'

I had learned the hard way that there is no substitute for daily waiting on God in order to know his empowering and infilling. Without personal prayer we are in serious trouble. I have often been asked if I am not afraid that it could happen again. I am mindful of Paul's words – 'Let anyone who thinks that he stands take heed lest he fall' (1 Corinthians 10.12) – but my fear is not so much for myself (I now know the danger and the signs) but for so many of my fellow ministers and church leaders who I suspect are making the same mistake.

I was out of the ministry for two and a half years. The church at Mitcham Lane supported us financially for several months and allowed us to stay in the manse until I had had a good rest, and then I worked in life assurance for nearly two years before accepting an invitation (with the blessing of the leaders of the denomination) to Teddington

Baptist Church, Middlesex, in 1982. Again, the church is growing steadily both numerically and spiritually and prayer is playing an increasingly important part. The same desire for prayer is growing up within the people, with much more prayer within our area house groups and church organisations. Prayer cells are springing up. In the leadership we are slowly learning to pray more and speak less! An emphasis on personal and family prayer is also stressed within the fellowship and we are beginning to reap the fruits of it.

We believe in prayer! Prayer is the Christian's vital breath. If we don't feel like praying we must pray until we do feel like praying. It is not as though there is no God there to help us! I believe that God is looking for men and women who, despite the problems, will fight through in God's strength to the place of victory in this area. It is vital. As Matthew Henry says, 'When God intends great mercy for His people, the first thing He does is set them a-praying.'

Freda Flude

Spirit-guided Prayer

Freda Flude has had an eventful life, knowing hardships and sorrows as well as joys, all of which have been used of the Lord in bringing her to an ever-deepening peace with himself. She has travelled in a number of countries and has also been involved in supplying Christian literature, mainly to the Spanish-speaking countries and India.

At present she is engaged in leading prayer conferences in various parts of England and the USA, for she has a burden concerning the need for prayer and intercession and for God's people to know the privilege and thrill and results of seeking him.

'Do you really mean, Lord, that my praying can change situations and lives?'

'Do you really mean, Lord, that my prayers can be "on target"?'

'Do you really mean that I can be so one with you that I will declare your word – found in prayer – that it might come to pass?'

'It is almost beyond my wildest dreams, Lord. I pray what you want prayed, I speak what you want spoken, I see what you want seen – and through me and my fellowship with you things happen.'

I feel I have found a pearl of great price and am ready to sell all that I had found in order to have this pearl.

If only I had realised earlier that my communion with the Lord was the most dynamic experience that anyone could have, my testimony and my Christian life would have been so different. If only I could now grasp the reality of the power generated from my day-to-day communion with the Lord, my day-to-day testimony would be so different.

However, what I have now seen and what I have now grasped has given me a goal – a goal that does not depend upon my natural status in this world, a goal that does not depend upon how many examinations I pass. This goal is not affected by my sex or my personality. One thing is required of me, and that is to give myself to fellowship with the Lord and to taking the time to listen to him in order to be guided by his Spirit.

After my initial experience of becoming a Christian and proving that the Lord hears and answers prayer, I seemed to go into such a dry period, where praying was almost a ritual and to attend a prayer meeting often meant at least one hour of boredom. Telling God the same thing over and over again, or asking him the same thing repeatedly, without any results, only made me want to avoid praying. Then I felt guilty. I knew not only that Christians should pray, but that they should want to pray. To have a prayer answered was a special event, and I could never understand why God occasionally answered a prayer and left all the others seemingly unheard.

Very slowly and very gradually I began to realise that my praying had to be guided praying. Just telling the Lord the details of a problem or a need resulted in my wondering whether he had heard me, whether he would do anything about it, and whether or not I had gone over the details sufficiently to persuade him that it needed his attention.

I now realise that some of my faulty concepts of prayer were a result of not fully believing that the Lord is always with me or realising that the power of the Holy Spirit was needed in my life. When I am aware of his presence I immediately respond and talk with him. When I learned to be quiet before him and listen to his voice instead of doing all the talking, I was lifted above the natural plane to a walk in the Spirit which I had not envisaged possible. Walking in faith in his word and in his guidance brings results beyond my comprehension.

One of my first awakening experiences regarding guidance in prayer, with results that amazed me, happened in England in 1970. I had been dusting my bedroom one morning and, feeling weary with the task, decided to sit down and pray in tongues. My decision was no different from when I decide to have a cup of coffee. I did not feel any particular desire to pray, I was not conscious of being led by the Lord – I was just feeling a little tired of housework.

It was also at a time in my life when I was learning to know the Lord's voice. As I prayed in tongues, one word came to my mind – 'Yorkshire'. I remember stopping and wondering why I should suddenly think of Yorkshire, for I had no friends or relatives in that county. I concluded that either my mind was making up something, or wandering, or it was the Lord speaking to me.

I decided to believe it was the Lord, and asked, 'Lord, why did you say Yorkshire? Is there anyone in need in Yorkshire, or is there going to be a revival there?'

I received nothing further from the Lord, so I made another decision, and said, 'Lord, I am going to pray in tongues again and I am going to believe that I am praying for Yorkshire, even though I do not understand why prayer is needed. I am going to believe that your Holy Spirit in me is doing something beyond my comprehension.'

I prayed in the Spirit, in tongues. I felt nothing, I did not see anything and I received no further word from the Lord. I did not spend long in prayer – no more than fifteen minutes – then I shrugged my shoulders and decided to continue my housework.

My surprise and reward and enlightenment came the next morning, for when I saw the newspaper the headline read 'Earth tremor in England'. The area worst affected was the north of Yorkshire, no one was hurt and there was only a little damage to some property.

I remember saying, 'So I *was* praying for Yorkshire.'

Dared I believe that no one was hurt because I had been in prayer? Dared I believe that it was only a small earth tremor that was felt and only slight damage had been caused because I prayed?

A similar experience came to me several years later. I was praying in tongues one evening, and again one word came to my mind. I use this expression because hearing the Lord's voice is not some way out spooky experience – it is not hearing a voice thundering from the heavens, it is not some special supernatural signal – it is just the Holy Spirit within me, who registers a thought which I could so easily brush aside as being just me, leaving me free to choose to believe that I am one with him in prayer and he is moving me and speaking to me.

The one word that came to me was 'Mozambique'.

Because of other experiences, I did not query that the Lord had spoken to me. I believed that I was in prayer for that country on the east coast of Africa. Again, I had no particular interest in Mozambique; I knew no one there, but was ready to work with the Lord in whatever he desired.

As I prayed, it was as if I had an inner knowledge that there were Christians in danger and this added impetus to my praying. Then I had what I so freely call a vision. I could also say that I imagined a scene, or that the Holy Spirit used my imagination and my thinking to channel what he wanted to show me.

I saw the camouflage material, which is used to make soldiers' uniforms when they are in battle. I felt a sense of urgency and, as I continued, I saw parachutists – which made me think that there was a spiritual battle going on and that spiritual reinforcements were needed; I certainly did not think there was a literal battle taking place.

Imagine my surprise and sense of wonder and awe when I heard the news that Mozambique had been raided by the South Africans and people had been killed. I could then only believe that my brothers and sisters in Christ had known protection because I had been in prayer.

I remember vividly that I had not felt any special constraint to pray. I had just decided to pray in tongues that evening, and in no way could I have prayed with my understanding.

I realise that I cannot understand with my mind the great variety of methods used by the Holy Spirit.

One morning, while having breakfast with a Swedish friend staying in my home, the postman brought a letter from Marta, a Swedish missionary in India. It was a heart-cry asking for prayer on her behalf, for she was very sick and would probably have to go into hospital for an operation. Marianne and I decided to seek the Lord immediately on behalf of Marta. So, with the remains of our meal still on the table, we began to pray in tongues.

After a while, the Lord said to me, 'Lay your hands upon

Marianne and pray for the healing of Marta in India.'

Still with my eyes closed, and realising that Marianne had stopped praying out loud, I pondered on what the Lord had said to me. I thought, Marianne will be standing in, or will be a substitute for Marta in India, and under the direction of the Holy Spirit the prayer of faith can be prayed. I opened my eyes to share this with Marianne and discovered that she did not look at all well, and had slumped against the wall where she was seated.

I asked, 'Are you all right, Marianne?'

'I feel ill,' she replied.

'But you were all right before we began to pray, weren't you?'

She answered, 'Yes, quite all right.'

Enlightenment came to me; she really was a substitute for Marta, for the sickness that was upon Marta was now being felt in her body.

I shared what the Lord had told me to do, and I stood up to fulfil the leading of the Holy Spirit. I laid my hands upon Marianne's head and prayed for the healing of Marta in India. Immediately the sick feeling that had come upon Marianne left her, and we knew that our faith and love had reached out to Marta and that by the power of the Holy Spirit she was restored. This was confirmed not long after by another letter from her.

On another occasion, when I was in India with Marta, pain developed in one of my legs. For two weeks I had been speaking twice a day in many villages and we were to have a day's holiday. We had planned to journey about seventy miles to the nearest large town, where we could do some shopping and spend the day free from any kind of work. We had been looking forward to this and I was rather dismayed when, the day before, this trouble developed in my leg.

I had to deliberately stop my mind from imagining the worst, for I began to wonder whether I had picked up some bug or had been bitten and there was poison affecting my leg. I did not know what to think and concluded that perhaps a good night's rest would deal with it, but when I lay down there was no more ease than when I was on my feet. In fact, my sleep that night was very restless, because I could not get my leg into a comfortable position.

We had to get up early to catch the six o'clock bus and I wished with all my heart that I did not have to make that journey. The day loomed ahead with much gloom. I did not want to disappoint Marta by not going, but I did not know how I was going to make the two journeys in the Indian bone-shakers and spend most of the day on my feet.

I had prayed for healing in my leg, but no change had taken place. I tried putting my leg in different positions on the bus to get ease, all to no effect. I again reached out to the Lord, and this time I said, 'Lord, do you have anything to say to me about this condition?'

Immediately the Lord said, 'Muriel'. It was as if I had suddenly become alert and alive. 'I see, Lord, Muriel in the fellowship at home is having trouble with her legs.'

It was not hard for me to understand this because at various times in the past she had had problems with her legs. Immediately I went into prayer on behalf of Muriel. I thanked the Lord for letting me feel the pain in my leg. I thanked him that he had let me have a bad night on behalf of my sister in England. Joy welled up within me, and my faith was ready to go into action. I prayed for the healing of Muriel's legs and thanked the Lord for doing it, and within minutes the pain left my leg.

What a day we had! It was doubly special, in spite of the dusty roads and the smells and the heat; it was our free day and Muriel's too.

I was one of a small group of people seeking the Lord one evening. During that time a young man spoke out and said that the Lord had brought to his mind a picture of an elephant. He had no idea why, and the Lord had not given him any reason for this. I have to confess that I thought, 'How ridiculous – anyone can picture an elephant in their mind's eye – and fancy being so stupid as to give it out without a meaning.'

There was a deadly silence in the room. No one took it

up, no one challenged it – in fact I do not think we really knew what to do with it. But ignoring it did not help the atmosphere.

After what seemed an interminable time, the silence was broken by another man in the group, asking us to pray for a minister whom he knew personally who was encountering much hardship and many problems in his church, to the extent that his health was being affected and so he had physical problems too. We were not given the name of the minister or the church involved, and we never did know for whom we were praying.

I think we were all glad to move on from the elephant, but as we prayed for this unknown minister I began to feel really sorry for the young man who had spoken out. I did not want him to be hurt or embarrassed, and, after all, in a small prayer group there should be room for adventure in prayer and room for mistakes to be made.

I just could not put my mind on the minister who was needing prayer, for it was upon the young man and what he had said. I realised there was only one thing I could do, I had to believe that he had received this picture from the Lord by the Holy Spirit.

I said, 'Lord, I am going to believe that you gave him that picture, and will you please give me the meaning and what you are conveying through the elephant.'

Immediately into my mind's eye came an elephant. I could see it so clearly, just as if I was at a zoo watching its movements. I saw its trunk go down to the ground and pick up some crumbs that had been thrown to it, and then I saw it pick up a bun and put the bun into its mouth. Then, as I waited on the Lord, I saw that same trunk carrying a huge tree that had been chopped down.

I said, 'What are you saying through this, Lord?'

Then he said to me, 'The minister for whom you are praying has the capacity in himself, which I have put within him, to feed from my word so that he is sustained; I have also given him the capacity to carry the heavy burden that is in his situation.'

I could have leapt for joy! So the young man was being led by the Holy Spirit! We could pray with definite purpose and in faith for this minister; and also we had a word from God to send to him.

I shared the interpretation of the vision and then we prayed, knowing that our prayer was on target for him to be healed and sustained and to carry the load that was upon him at that time.

The word of God was delivered by the friend who had requested prayer, and I could only imagine how I would have felt if I had been in that minister's shoes, receiving a direct message from God that he was strengthened for the purpose and the situation he was in, and need not fear or be depressed or affected physically.

I learned very much through that incident. The Lord still takes simple things and uses them to speak to us. He used the lily of the field, the sower sowing seed, and he can take an elephant to channel our minds and our faith. I also realised that before we called he had answered with a word for this minister.

While staying with some friends in Germany, I was asked to join a church group that was visiting a prison and to give a word to the prisoners. I accepted, in spite of having only one day's notice. I did not make a special effort to withdraw myself from my friends to seek the Lord in a concentrated way on behalf of the prisoners.

I reaped what I sowed – or, I should say, I did not reap because I had not sown – for I knew that I did not get anything over to this fairly large group of young men in their teens and early twenties and I knew that the power of the Holy Spirit was not in action.

About a year later, I was in the United States of America and was asked if I would speak in a mission for down and outs. I agreed, and immediately determined that I would not have the result that I had had in Germany. Admittedly, this time I had about one week to pray and I told the Lord in no uncertain terms that I was not going to have the same results, for it was not worth my going to speak unless he could do something through me for those down and outs. I did not want to go and speak just for the sake of speaking – I wanted results for his glory and for his Kingdom.

I had no idea what the people would be like who attended this meeting, but I began praying and loving them before the Lord. I tried to put myself into their shoes, imagining what their lifestyles might have been like. Maybe some had not known the love and care of good parents, maybe some had had broken marriages and broken homes, maybe some had gone into crime and drugs. I also thought much about God's love; I knew that he loved each one of them and wanted to draw them to himself, to rescue them from their sin and their misery.

I arrived at the Mission about half an hour before the meeting was due to start, and with four other friends went into a very small adjoining room to pray. I began to weep – a weeping that seemed to be uncontrollable; as the tears flowed I felt such love and compassion, and at the same time such misery and sorrow. My companions felt it wise to leave me alone in prayer and it was as much as I could do to mop my face and pull myself together by the start of the meeting.

When I walked into the room in which the meeting was held I could hardly believe my eyes, for I had never been in a situation like this one before. There were old men who looked like tramps and there were young men whose heads were hanging down, obviously on drugs.

The treasurer of the church with which I was in fellow-ship led the meeting and chose old familiar hymns, hoping that at least some of the old men might remember them from their boyhood days. He seemed surprised when two or three of them started to join in the singing, and said, 'It is so lovely of you to help us – you have not done this before.' This was an encouragement to my faith, and when called upon I gave the message that the Lord had given me for this motley bunch.

To my amazement the heads that were hanging down became upright as I gave a love message from our Father. It was a thrilling moment for me when I made an appeal for those who wanted to respond to God's love and to know the Lord Jesus as their Saviour, and eight – young and old – stood immediately from this small group. The workers at the Mission were surprised at the response and I could see how God's love could penetrate and what working together with the Lord in prayer could do. I could see how the power of the Holy Spirit could flow through an ordinary individual to touch shipwrecked lives.

The demands of life and the pressure of this modern age so often invade the time when we would pray. I remember pouring my heart out to the Lord one day about my situation, telling him that I did want to seek him, I did want to pray, but there were so many other things needing my attention. Legitimate things – letters to be answered, many of which needed prayer even for the answer – telephone calls, and people coming to my home – all of these, apart from my own personal family needs and the shopping and cleaning and the everyday chores that had to be carried out.

I said, 'Lord, I just do not know what to leave and everything seems to demand attention. The one thing that I know is vital so often gets squeezed out and I am often too tired at the end of the day to make the effort to pray.'

The Lord immediately gave me a picture in my mind of Tower Bridge in London. I saw it beginning to open up in order to let a large ship through, and I saw that all the traffic that constantly flows over the bridge had to wait until the ship had passed through and the bridge was accessible again. It did not matter how urgent or how important were the journeys of those people in the cars and buses, they had to wait.

I knew the Lord was saying to me that there are times when all other things have to wait, however important those things may be.

On another occasion I was sharing with a group of ladies in a church in India. I had felt I should encourage them in prayer and had been telling them how the Lord is interested even in the small details of our lives, and how our walk and talk with the Lord can be so natural.

I told them about an incident when I had been praying about new curtains for my daughter's bedroom, and that he had shown me to make them twelve inches longer than the previous ones that had been at the window. I had been suspecting that we might be moving at a later stage, and thought the Lord was telling me to make them longer so they would fit windows in a different house. I had no idea that the curtains would last so well, and would still be in perfect condition when a number of years later the colour scheme of the room was changed. It was a great delight to me to discover that a member of the prayer group was needing fresh curtains of the exact shade of these which I no longer wanted in my home. However, if they had not been made twelve inches longer they would not have fitted her windows.

Then I told them about a visit I made to a minister's wife in the heart of the country. When I had been looking to the Lord about my visit, he had told me to take her some bananas: I obeyed, and on my arrival told her what the Lord had instructed me to do. She was thrilled because, being unable to drive a car and living miles from any shops, she could only buy their groceries and supplies when her husband or a member of the family was able to take her to the nearest village. She had been taken that morning but had forgotten the bananas that she needed.

I also shared with these ladies in India that when my mother had been seriously ill and we were expecting her to die, I had obeyed God's word where it says, 'They shall lay hands on the sick and they shall recover' (Mark 16.18, AV). I had done this in fear and trembling but my mother's faith had reached out to God and she was miraculously healed.

I had been recounting these and other incidents of what I had discovered in prayer – sharing that God wants to use us as channels of prayer on behalf of others and that he uses us to be the answers to other people's prayers too. I threw the meeting open to any questions, and, to my dismay, the first lady who stood up requested me to pray for the healing of

149

her fifteen-year-old daughter who had been born mentally handicapped. All of a sudden I wished I had not opened the meeting up for questions, and, more than that, I wished I had not talked about God answering prayer! There was nothing I could do but to pray for the healing of that girl, asking the Lord to heal her, to deal with the defects and to bring her into normality. I endeavoured to focus my attention on the Lord rather than on the situation and the people watching me.

I inwardly heaved a sigh of relief when the meeting was ended and it was time for light refreshments. I sat alone sipping a cup of Indian tea, when the minister came to my side and said the mother had asked if I would be willing to go to her home and see the girl. That sort of question puts me in a spot – would I be willing to go? Yes, I was willing to go, but on the other hand, it was the last place I wanted to go.

I agreed to make this visit, but was amazed to discover that practically everyone else made their way along the rough pathway to this Indian home. I was totally unprepared for this. It seemed as though the whole village had turned out! The children climbed up at the glassless windows and many entered into the room where the girl was seated, while others thronged round the doorway – expecting something to happen because of this white woman's presence.

The girl was seated in a chair, rocking backwards and forwards, and yelling to the point of almost screaming. I had no idea whether this was her normal condition or whether she was disturbed by my presence and the presence of the crowd. I asked if some of the people could be removed from the room, but that made little difference to the girl's reaction. Reaching out to the Lord, I asked him if this girl was demon-possessed. I knew I was out of my depth and had no idea what I was dealing with or what was required of me. The Lord did not say anything to me, or perhaps I was so conscious of my surroundings that he spoke without my hearing him. But because I had not heard anything, I did not attempt to do anything, except to pray again the prayer I had prayed in the church – asking the Lord to heal the girl.

When I departed I left the girl in the same plight that she was in when I arrived, and looking back I see the wisdom of God, for not one of those villagers could attribute any magic power to me.

Nearly a week later I was in another village and met two ladies who had been at the meeting. Marta, my Swedish missionary friend, immediately asked the ladies how this girl was getting on. I groaned inwardly, just wishing she had kept quiet. I was not going to ask any questions; I was almost afraid to do so. I was amazed at the thrilling news, for these women declared that the girl, who was normally so noisy, had become much calmer. Also they related how, though the mother had always had difficulty in persuading her daughter to eat, the girl had now started asking for food.

My faith soared at this information and I immediately gave the two ladies a message for the mother, telling her not to settle for the improvement as the total answer to the prayer. Neither was she to look to the girl for further evidence of improvement. If she did the healing would stop – for it would then be a looking for evidence to believe rather than believing in God's answer and seeing the evidence come to pass through faith. When I visited the area one year later I was told that this girl had made continued progress throughout the year.

Praying is wonderful and it is an adventure. There is not a fixed pattern or formula – if there were we would have had it in operation a long time ago. Effective praying is a result of being a pupil and learning obedience; being a son and learning to know and understand the Father; being an ambassador and spokesman and knowing the directorship of the Holy Spirit in the name of our Lord Jesus Christ.

Douglas McBain

Prophetic Praying

Douglas McBain is Director of Manna Ministries Trust which aims to co-operate with the Holy Spirit in the renewal of the Church. He has been a Baptist Minister for twenty-five years, the last fourteen of which were at Streatham Baptist Church, Lewin Road. During that time the process of inner urban decline was arrested and the church experienced much renewal and growth. His new ministry takes him overseas and also spans the spectrum of many different church traditions. His wife, Christine, works with him. Together they are involved in church planting in Chelsea.

The children, Alison and her husband Alec Swift, Elspeth, Janet and Graham give valued support.

She was no more than about four feet six inches tall and of a frail physique. In spite of this she managed to hold a packed congregation spellbound with the exciting story of her work for God which had been brought to an abrupt and premature end. Nor did she send us away from the church door with a bland 'Goodnight, God bless you.' Fixing each of us in turn with her bright brown eyes she gave a final exhortation from the sermon she had just preached to 'Pray for China'.

Gladys Aylward was an expert communicator of her own passionate commitment to the work of Christ in China. The Church was entering the early years of persecution following the Communist take-over of 1949. Subsequent events have shown the great significance of the prayer for China that she advocated. Far from dying out because of the intense hardships, prayer has been miraculously answered. For the Chinese Church today is experiencing an astonishing growth and thrilling vitality which its trials have only served to encourage. As has often been the case when God has moved in mighty reviving power, it is as if the Holy Spirit has been adding a few further chapters to the thrilling story of the Book of Acts.

This encounter with Gladys Aylward remains one of my earliest memories of Christian things after my boyhood conversion. The prophetic dimension of prayer which lies behind it is one to which I have frequently returned. Paul urges us to make use of many different ways of praying. 'And pray in the Spirit on all occasions *with all kinds of prayer and requests*. With this in mind, be alert and always keep on praying for all the saints' (Ephesians 6.18, italics mine). However, this element of prophetic praying in which we open our minds in order to hear God as much as we open our mouths in order to address him, is a kind of praying which lies close to the heart of prayer. It reminds us that as in every other aspect of Christian experience the initiative in prayer is God's.

This was one of the lessons that God the Father impressed upon the disciples of Jesus more than once throughout his earthly ministry. 'This is my beloved Son . . . Listen to Him' (Matthew 17.5). To fail to hear him speak or to misunderstand what he is saying may well have been as recurrent a problem for them as it so frequently is for us. Yet it is those who most want to hear his voice who will be most keen to learn to listen. The times when God's people pray then become the times when he speaks most clearly to them.

God Speaks First

God speaks to his people in prayer in order that we may enjoy an intimate relationship with him. When this happens as the whole church gathers together there is always a fresh infusion of power and also a fresh sense of corporate direction.

It happened like this for us in the early days of spiritual renewal in the church in Streatham. We had received a prayer request for the healing of quite a number of our own church children, and had already discovered that children are apparently more able to receive a healing ministry than older people. This opens up many intriguing issues for us. On this occasion things were critical. The child was seriously ill and in a coma condition with encephalitis. His life was hanging in the balance. If he recovered, then the prognosis was very poor. The child's parents were not committed Christians although they were God-fearers.

Since our faith certainly did not match the seriousness of the condition we fell into the error of thinking that maybe we could improve the quality of our praying by increasing its quantity and so we arranged special times of prayer.

This was to no avail. There was no improvement in Daren's condition at all until one of our ladies came to us with God's word. She regularly prayed and as regularly admitted to having problems with faith in the process. Nevertheless, the word God gave to her was crystal clear: 'The Lord says that Daren is to be healed now,' she declared. It was not an expression of a general hope that he might get better but a confident declaration from one whose spiritual reliability was clear that healing had come. And so it turned out. The boy was instantly healed. To our joy and that of his parents he has never looked back and he is now a fully fit six-footer without any trace of the illness at all.

In a similar way, we heard God speak to us quite clearly on another occasion when we were praying together for healing for two of our own Christian family. Connie was my right hand helper but was diagnosed as suffering with inoperable cancer. Bob was a bright young Christian who had just finished his studies at university and was apparently ill with a bad attack of appendicitis. The Lord told us quite plainly that he would take Connie home and heal Bob, but we got the message confused because of our natural desire for healing for both of them. As the Lord's word was fulfilled, Connie's experience became a powerful demonstration of how Christians full of the Holy Spirit can greet death as a friend and not a foe. Bob's healing was no less powerful. He had been suffering from Crohn's disease and salmonella poisoning as well as appendicitis, and for a while his life, too, hung in the balance. As the healing came to him, it became clear to us that the Lord had fulfilled his own word. He was also deepening our corporate dependence on him.

This openness to God is the foundation on which the ministry of intercession rests. It underpins every prayer of faith. It can also inspire militant prayers in which we carry the battle to the mighty strongholds of the enemy. At the invitation of the Lord there is a loving friendship for us to enjoy with Christ, through which we share our innermost secrets with him and he shares with us his least publicised purposes. As a consequence his will is no longer a closely guarded secret. 'I no longer call you servants because a servant does not know his master's business,' says Jesus. 'Instead, I have called you friends, for everything I have learned from my Father I have made known to you' (John 15.15).

Hearing and Going

From my own perception, the Church's ministry of healing can only be effectively exercised within this understanding of an articulate Lord who is willing to speak clearly to his people. God's word to us personally will also be on a similar basis. It was because of this that in 1976 I found myself ministering the gospel many thousands of miles away from home in a remote mountain village called Dupax on the island of Luzon in the Philippines. The plans for my overseas tour of ministry had been coming together gradually throughout the preceding year, and my church had given me leave of absence in order to engage in it.

Two months before I left I was due to speak at a special day's conference at Ashburnham Place in Sussex. I had been fulfilling a very heavy pastoral schedule and the result was that I had set out for that day's ministry tired, under-rested, and without having spent adequate time in prayer and preparation. It had been a tough day there, too, with an awkward group of ministers and clergy who were thoroughly jaded and problem orientated. The weather suited my own depressed mood because the sun never shone through the November gloom and drizzle.

At last, at about four in the afternoon, they gave me a break and I was able to escape into privacy for a short while. I felt I needed fresh air and prayer and then some sleep. I combined the first two priorities by a quiet walk around the lake at Ashburnham. As I was tramping around the water's edge I heard an almost audible instruction to look up. I obeyed and saw that for the first time on that miserable day there was a break in the low-lying cumulus. It did my heart good to see it and so I thanked God and went on with my prayer recreation. Again I heard the same voice. By now the break in the clouds had broadened and several early evening stars were twinkling through it, making a glorious contrast to the dullness all around them. Again I thanked God for the sight, which I sensed had a great significance, though what it was I did not know. So after a snooze in a quiet lounge we came to the evening meeting. In the worship, before I spoke, one after another stood up to comment on those stars shining through the clouds. It seemed as if they had all the inspired wisdom of the Psalmist, Abraham and St John the Divine, but none of them helped me to understand what God was saying to me personally.

It was not until the next day that things became clear. As I shared this experience with another Christian friend, he had the interpretation for what had been a vision in prayer: 'The President's flag of the Philippines has a crescent of stars on it. When you go to South-East Asia in a few months' time would you preach there with some of my friends?' he asked.

I gladly agreed that this was from God and so found myself some months later in the mountain villages teaching and evangelising. When one of the national pastors asked me how God had called me to this brief experience I had no difficulty in explaining things to them. Some of my church members back at home were surprised and even distressed to see their pastor including this work in his busy overseas tour; after all, it was based upon a flimsy word received whilst praying in Sussex, but the Filipino pastors did not share that difficulty.

'I am here because God called me through those stars,' I said in answer to their questions. We were standing on the open verandah of a little home in the middle of a jungle clearing. Around us were beautifully perfumed trees bearing exotic fruit. From all over that district people were coming together for our meeting and several were coming in order to find the power of Christ to save and to heal. As I answered the pastors' questions, they needed no further explanation. As Christians with a different and more scriptural understanding in this respect they knew well that the Lord to whom we speak is the One who clearly responds to us if we have ears to hear him.

The Scriptures make it clear to us that it is this issue of hearing God speak to us which resolves all our problems in discovering God's will for our lives. If guidance is difficult, the answer lies in developing an effective prayer life. The experience of Peter, Paul and John in the New Testament confirms that this is so. Jesus declares it to us in the clearest terms as the great secret behind the whole of his ministry: 'The Son can do nothing by himself; he can do only what he sees his Father doing, because whatever the Father does the Son also does. For the Father loves the Son and shows him all that he does' (John 5.19). The word he gives can be expressed pictorially in the mind as well as audibly in the ear.

It would be a strange teaching indeed that made out the Father denied to his ordinary present day children what he clearly gave to his special Son Jesus. Not only strange teaching but bad doctrine. For we too will hear his voice and receive his word (John 10.27). It is this that confirms to us that we are his children and he is our Good Shepherd. To hear him speak rescues our praying from the living death of a monotonous litany of words. Instead of this it becomes the attractive centrepiece at the heart of our personal devotion. This is not to deny that there are other aspects to prayer, but it is to get their importance in perspective. For nothing is so stimulating as to hear him share his thoughts and speak his word. It is one thing for God to hear our voice, it is much more important that we hear his.

David's experience described in 2 Samuel 7 encourages us particularly when we face difficulties here. Can we disentangle his words from the multitude of spiritual soundwaves that strike our inner ears? Our own ideas can so easily intrude and attempt a take-over bid on what God is saying. This is the reason why advance is often halted even in churches which have established trail-blazing reputations as leaders in the matters of spiritual life. It is not just individual Christians who make mistakes here. Like David, groups of Christians have arrived at their pre-arranged plan of how to proceed with a due sense of their own priorities. Like David, too, they are never content unless they have apparently received divine sanction for schemes that God has never planned but which suit their own ideas.

It took a clear-minded Nathan to set David to rights about his desire to build a new sanctuary. And it is often like that for us, too. God's revealed plan for David dwarfed his own personal understanding and it astonished him. He had thought about a building scheme which his son Solomon would complete. God was speaking to him about his family, his throne, his kingdom, his dynasty and ultimately other nations also: 'Is this your usual way of dealing with man, O Sovereign Lord?' exclaimed David. Yes, the Scriptures confidently reply. For God's thoughts and his ways are above and beyond our own. Yet to seek him and to spend time with him is to come to the place where the secret plans are made known and the hidden truths revealed. Ever since Adam and Eve fell, this is what God has been longing for from sinful man. Responsiveness to him is the first sure sign of grace received. It is the promise of a vital relationship to come.

Other Voices

There are many ways by which we can check out that the voice we hear is God's and not that of another. We cannot ignore the activity of the enemy. He appears like an alien ventriloquist using as his dummy a snake in the garden of Eden (Genesis 3.1), a lion to Peter (1 Peter 5.8) and an angel of light to Paul (2 Corinthians 11.14). He can even use an apostle, like Peter, for the same purpose. He knows no more satisfying conquest than to pick up the pious in their prayers. Having confused the chasing of fantasies with hearing God, their prayer life becomes a hopeless meander without wisdom or goal.

But Christ's word to us will always harmonise with his

character as the Holy Spirit has depicted it in Scripture. His words will express his heart. For it is as true for God as it is for us that 'Out of the abundance of the heart the mouth speaks' (Matthew 12.34, RSV). These words will communicate his presence and affirm his sets of values. They will be confirmed by the whole tenor of his revelation through Scripture. Even when his words to us are personal they will be authenticated by the experience of God's saints from Abraham onwards.

The subjective test is in that ring of truth which we perceive. If the word is God's then those who receive it do not need to strive for its fulfilment. Even as they receive the word they enjoy peace and a quiet composure of heart and mind. More than that, God's word to them will open them up to stimulating responsiveness. Prophetic praying involves a two-way conversation between a loving Lord and his attentive people. Having heard God speak they know how to reply and what to ask God for.

Answering God
Our first response when God speaks to us must always be one of thanksgiving and praise. This has been one of the many refreshing discoveries characterising churches which have been affected by the worldwide movement of the Holy Spirit in recent years. Nor have the expressions of praise been confined within the covers of recently revised hymnals. God's people have been enjoying singing new songs to the Lord. Many of these songs are only of temporary value and will pass away. Some of them vividly express such strong scriptural truth that they are destined to have a long term effectiveness in the praise of the whole church. I have known charismatic advocates who have become indignant at the way in which their songs have found their way into the praise of other Christians, but I do not agree with this viewpoint. Rather, for me it is a confirmation of the validity of the experience that first gave birth to the song. If God has inspired the praise even the most distant members of his far flung family will sense a

response to it. In the Anglican liturgy it is a phrase which follows the reading of the Gospel that expresses this best.

'This is the Gospel of Christ,' says the Reader.

'Praise to Christ our Lord,' reply the people.

Not that this always harmonises with our own shared experience, but it is what we hope for and genuinely move towards. In Streatham the times of open prayer and praise in the regular services were often times when God spoke to us very distinctly. Sometimes they were also occasions which seemed tailor-made for the raucous interjection of the undisciplined. I think of an open-air preacher who came to our services but was not a member of the church. I shudder to think what effect his powerful pronouncements about the nearness of the day of judgment must have had upon those with frayed nerves or confused minds. We always knew when he had shown up by the distinctive bellow which broke up our praise and I knew that my sermon was in for a stormy time ahead, but even so, I could not find it in me to be deeply offended. His sparkling eyes peered out through thick-lensed spectacles and from an impish face. Of course his mistake was simply to confuse noise with power, and personal pleasure with spiritual freedom. He would have been a better man and probably a better preacher had he learned modulation in all things.

Creation calls the Christian with the same voice as Redemption. As the black Judean hills turned to purple, then orange, then gold in the light of another new day, David sang, 'Awake my soul! Awake, harp and lyre! I will awaken the dawn. I will praise you . . . your faithfulness reaches to the skies' (Psalm 57.8–9). Like David we too, who have received God's grace and his love, cry out with joyful gratitude to our Creator for the day that we are entering.

The Spirit helps us pray. Praise is a platform for worship. It is also a doorway for Spirit-inspired intercession. It is the work of the Holy Spirit to initiate God's advance to us. It is also the work of the Holy Spirit to stimulate all our responses. Paul says, 'We do not know how we ought to pray but the Spirit himself intercedes for us with groans that words cannot express. And he who searches our hearts, knows the mind of the Spirit, because the Spirit intercedes for the saints in accordance with God's will' (Romans 8.26–27).

Often this work of the Spirit is expressed through sharp perceptions of the needs of others, which are otherwise quite unknown to us. It was like that on one occasion for my family at home when I was away in Christian ministry in an inaccessible part of South-East Asia. When I am away like this I always feel some personal tension until I have re-established communication with my family through the sending and receiving of mail. On this occasion that flimsy link had been made but for no clear reason had subsequently broken down. No doubt somewhere in a dusty mailbag in a darkened corner of an airport building there lay these crumpled contact points between us. So back at home they prayed and they wrote yet again to another forwarding address. As they prayed, it was a West Indian friend who received and communicated the assurance they needed: 'I can see Douglas surrounded by a sea of friendly faces. Lots of people carrying lanterns are around him. He is all right. They are all smiling,' said Espy. Then, just a short while later, came the next stage. Through another visual image they saw a dammed-up river suddenly bursting its banks. As the water poured through the breach it scoured out the refuse of the river valley ready for a fresh and healthy harvest that would come subsequently.

That was the message that eventually came through to me where I was. The first was not of immediate significance since I knew that I was all right. But it was important for them. But the second intrigued me. That very morning I had been taken to see a sight that was the same as the scene that the Spirit-led friends had received earlier in England. It meant only one thing. Clearly God was going to bless there in ways far beyond our expectations. And so he did that night. Crowds gathered to hear God's word, all of them carrying a torch or bearing a lantern, and the Holy Spirit brought many of them to Christ for healing and salvation.

On other occasions the Holy Spirit moves his people to pray in tongues, that is with words in a language which we cannot immediately recognise or translate. This experience has been the source of endless Christian discussion. Sometimes it has provoked quite needless Christian division, with some claiming far too much for it, while others have denied that it has any worth or validity. Plainly the practice does not originate from normal thought processes. Concerning the tongues speaker Paul says, 'No one understands him; he utters mysteries with his spirit' (1 Corinthians 14.2). Equally plainly this in itself does nothing to invalidate it. As with some forms of poetry and music, there is another factor at work here. The language of tongues emerges out of our spirits as they are gifted by the Holy Spirit. Like the power of intuition, such an expression conveys its own validity as much by its sound as by its content.

To say that it always conveys the element of surprise when we hear it is perhaps to state the obvious. It was never more surprising than one Wednesday night in our church hall in Streatham, when the effect was almost like a tiny microcosm of the Day of Pentecost. Even on this occasion, as is often the way with these things, the full impact and meaning was not at first apparent for it was only after the meeting was concluded that a Nigerian Muslim who had attended came to ask me where this fellow countryman was who had spoken that night in the prayer time. It took a moment for me to grasp the significance of his question. There were no other Nigerians present that night. But what had happened was that the message in tongues had come to this man in the language of a Nigerian tribe that was a neighbour to his own. As a result he opened up to hear the message of Christ and made a positive response. In that meeting the church had been praying about its evangelism and the Spirit had chosen to make the very act of prayer an occasion for its own fulfilment. For all the exposure we have had to this particular form of praying, I do not think we have yet come to an adequate valuation of it. God has things to teach us about prayer in the Spirit of which tongues is a primary lesson. We need to go on to learn much more as our spirits respond to his Spirit in this way.

Practising the Art of Prayer
We face a formidable range of problems in the practice of prayer that threaten to keep us from it. In spite of our recognition of its priority we all too easily allow the pressures of a busy life and crowded timetable to keep us from praying. My wife is a better disciplined person at prayer than I am. An itinerant style of ministry does not help. I often have to battle against a form of spiritual inertia. The trivia can so easily absorb the time. There will certainly be no telephones in heaven to disturb our communion there!

I find that the greatest difficulty is caused through times of spiritual dryness in which God's absence is more evident than his Presence. To make my prayer life into a thing of duty is to kill it. To keep a prayer life without an element of self-discipline is equally destructive. I find it necessary both to make time and to take time for praying, as if my very life depends upon it. In a very real sense it does. So the time spent is never wasted and the effort required pays handsome dividends.

I find it personally helpful to go to prayer with the aid of a Bible, a notebook and a biro. Oh for editions of the Bible with legible print, and india paper that can take fluorescent underlinings! Just a cheap notebook is valuable to write down what we believe God is saying. 'The palest ink is stronger than the weakest memory,' says the Chinese proverb. Through this method many a gentle hope has enlarged into a clear vision and many clearly conceived plans have been formulated. We need to move out of general sloganising about spiritual aims and into spiritual strategies, and we can do this if we go to God with a pen.

For God equips his people with authority in prayer. Our enemy is like the snake with venom in his mouth and the scorpion with the sting in his tail. But Jesus has given us the right to stand upon Satan and trample him under foot (Luke 10.19). We need to be effectively anointed and fully equipped if our service is to be crowned with success. Such an ambition is a characteristic of our age and a badge for Christian activists. The paradox is that we can only really achieve anything for God by doing things his way. Far from our prayer life then becoming a retreat into internalised contemplations in which we achieve nothing, it becomes, according to Jesus, the moment of dynamic release. For the Christ of history is at the Father's side (John 14.12). Through our praying he breaks forth afresh into the new situation we now present before him. The result is transformation. In prophetic praying God will have first spoken to us. Our response will be with the swift recall of an active memory and the vivid imagination of an inspired faith. It will not be a substitute for action, but rather an expression of it. The inspiration for this is God's but the action is ours. That is the glory of prayer. It is the God-given means by which we find God for ourselves and establish a relationship with him. And in the process of discovering God – we also find ourselves.

Dr Anne Townsend

Prayer: When God Seems Far Away

Dr Anne Townsend was born in London, and trained at the Royal Free Hospital. She and her husband, John, served as missionaries in Thailand for sixteen years during the sixties and seventies. They have a daughter 'Beff' (twenty-two) and two sons David (twenty) and 'Ditch' (eighteen).

Anne was editor of *Family* and took up a new appointment as a director of CARE Trust (Christian Action Research in Education) in Autumn 1984.

John is a surgeon. He is in full-time Christian service with TEAR Fund. He is based in the UK but travels widely.

I sat alone one January afternoon, six years ago, on the downs of Ditchling Beacon. It was cold and I huddled into my shawl for extra warmth. I had fled the family for a couple of hours to be alone, to think and pray about the future. That afternoon was my fortieth birthday, and I did not want to be forty! I didn't feel forty, and I didn't like the thought that half my life was already over. I did not want to be middle-aged, old and past it. The biting wind pierced my coat, a blanket of rain swept over the fields below me, and for some reason I could not identify I felt frozen to the marrow. Sitting, musing on being forty, I was suddenly frightened. I sensed that something was going to happen to me, and I was not going to enjoy it. Whatever it was, it would be painful.

In my dread I could sense the presence of God, and it was as if he was clearly speaking to me and saying, 'Something is going to happen, and you have a choice to make now that will affect your future. You can choose now either to follow me through the future, or to go your own way and ignore me.' For some inexplicable reason I found this choice hard. Although I had then been a Christian for twenty-six years my immediate response was not an automatic, 'Lord, I'll follow you till I die.' My sense of foreboding was such that I could only pray haltingly, and slowly at first, 'Lord, whatever happens I want to follow you to the end . . . .'

Now, later, when I remember that afternoon and am tempted to tell myself that I was imagining things, I remind myself that such was my sense of God's Presence (and some kind of fear about the future) that on returning home I went straight upstairs and changed my clothes to remove all reminder of that awesome afternoon.

A week later I began to know why God had given me the choice of deciding whether to follow him or not – no matter what happened. It was the beginning of six months that was to change me as a person and as a Christian. During that six months I was shattered to the core. Five close friends were killed in a road accident together with their seven children; my husband had a small cancer removed from his face (small in size but major in the anxiety it caused me); I was one of the two last people to talk to a very special Christian man before he was killed on the motorway; my husband's father developed a brain haemorrhage and died after a few months; I fell downstairs and knocked myself out and broke my arm; I had a virus infection in my ear that made me too giddy to walk . . . plus other major happenings in my life that affected me deeply.

During those six months and for another three years afterwards I learned one of the most important lessons of my pilgrimage as a Christian – how to go on walking with God even when he seems to be absent. One week after my fortieth birthday I felt totally cut off from God and could no longer sense his presence or his reality – and that hurt. Experiencing God as real in my own being was something very important to me, and this experience of being unable to sense God lasted for three and a half years!

I had never understood before what people were talking about when they spoke of a 'wilderness experience' – now I knew. In those three and a half years I felt desolate, alone and cut off from God, and I then knew what 'the wilderness' could be like.

The fact that on my birthday I had consciously pledged to God that I would follow him no matter what happened, was important to me. In my darkness and inability to feel God, I was able to tell myself, 'You said that you would go on following and to do that you now have to walk as a Christian regardless of your emotions.' And so I set my will to live as a Christian.

Prayer in 'the wilderness' took on a different dimension. I prayed because I was determined to go on following Jesus –

but being unable to sense him there when I prayed made it hard to worship from the heart. I tried to be faithful in praying, and simply to ask as I had always asked in the past. Prayer became for me, during those years, a very simple matter of being a child trusting its father. I had to come to God to say that I believed he would be true to his word, that he wouldn't let me down, that I couldn't do anything without him and I needed his help all the time.

Prayer was also very much a case of leaning back in God's arms when I felt bruised, hurt and bewildered, and reassuring myself that no matter how I felt, God's loving arms were round me. I could be assured of that because it said so in the Bible. I could trust – when I could not feel – that 'underneath were God's everlasting arms'. And when I felt as if I was falling down, down, down into a very deep pit, I told myself as I tried to pray that wherever I was falling God's safe strong arms were waiting to catch me and stop me from smashing myself at the bottom.

Continually I had to remind myself that on my birthday I had decided of my own free will to go on with God, and continually I had to set my will actually to do this.

During those three and a half years I shared myself with no one. I was too hurt and too vulnerable to expose my raw wounds even to friends. I went on existing, and I assume that to onlookers I was functioning as a Christian but inside I felt as if I were frozen.

Because I had written a book about intercessory prayer, *Prayer without Pretending,* people seemed to assume that I was some kind of expert on prayer – but during those wilderness years I was expert only at clinging on when the little light in my darkness seemed fast to be disappearing.

To maintain my integrity I had, in those years, to refuse the many invitations I received to speak at meetings about prayer. How could I – for whom prayer had ceased to be joyous and full of meaning – possibly go round speaking from platforms about prayer? I didn't tell anyone the reasons why I wouldn't speak at their meetings. My confusion about what was happening inside left me unsure and tongue-tied. I was very afraid that if anyone really knew what I was like I would be rejected and unloved by fellow Christians. Their acceptance of me was important in recovering from the bereavement I faced from the deaths of my five friends and their seven children.

I cannot pin-point any special factors that brought me out again from those wilderness years. It was as if my frozenness gradually thawed over a period of months. It didn't happen quickly but gradually. Without my noticing it, I realised my sense of awareness of God was returning. I would hear a bird singing, and stop to listen for the first time for years, and listening, find I was instinctively worshipping the One who created bird song. I would see a snowdrop piercing the snow and be aware of the pristine beauty – and from nowhere I sensed God close by me in the snow. Gradually, a sense that God was there again crept on me unawares at unexpected moments until, after many months, it seemed that my sensitivity to God had been restored. I could again sense him in ways I had almost forgotten, and had begun to assume were of the past and were never to be restored to me.

During the three years of walking in the wilderness my husband and I had returned to England, after sixteen years of living and working as missionaries in Thailand. When we returned six years ago it was to an England that was different from the land we had left as young idealistic doctors. The pace of life had quickened and everything seemed strangely different.

At first I struggled just to be a British housewife and run a home – a role I had never assumed since we had married, as we had always lived overseas. Then I struggled to cope with a busy career as well as run a home – for as missionaries returning to Britain and approaching middle-age we found that we both had to work to earn sufficient to start buying a house and support three teenage children.

Soon I was a busy career woman who could spend all her evenings speaking at meetings if she didn't watch out! I thrived on my new job as editor of *Family* – gladly working overtime if necessary as I enjoyed the job so much.

I adapted to the kind of Christianity I saw in Britain, a Christianity that was rather different from what I had been used to as a missionary with the Overseas Missionary Fellowship. I was accustomed to top priority being given to days of prayer. The hospital in which I had worked as a doctor regularly ran on a skeleton staff so that the rest could attend prayer days. I was used to people who regarded prayer as vital to anything and everything, and who soaked their lives in prayer.

When we returned to Britain five years ago we returned to a land of instant everything—instant coffee, instant meals, instant success and apparently instant spirituality. I was attracted by the bright, warm effervescent type of Christianity I saw. I liked the people and felt one with them.

I listened to what some of them had to say and was attracted—although I should not have been! I heard them say—and I may have been wrong in my perception of their words—that as Christians we were no longer under law but under grace. That sounded biblical to me! I couldn't disagree. They went on to say that as we were free, then we were free to enjoy God and to pray to him at any time. We didn't need to feel bound to set the alarm and get up in the morning early to be with him—we could be with him at any time of the day.

I agreed with this and liked the sound of it. In my forties I was rethinking old assumptions, and trying to discover who I was now that I had almost finished my role as mother. I was also walking blind and frozen in a spiritual wilderness, and wondered if freedom from old disciplines might lead me into the life I lacked.

I saw others experiencing God in a way that I couldn't, in an apparent spiritual high at meetings, and was attracted to this instant, seeming spirituality. I rarely made time in the mornings to pray and study God's word, and genuinely tried to find other times at other parts of the day. This worked sometimes. But at the end of a couple of years I looked at myself long and hard in a period of painful assessment and realised that the total number of hours I had spent with God was a thimbleful when compared with the oceans of time I had spent with the television set.

I saw that, for me, the only answer to being with God was to make time to spend with him – and in my life that had to be early in the morning. It was a conscious decision to go back to the old disciplines of getting up early enough to pray and read my Bible before leaving for work – rather than hoping that somehow I'd find time for God in a day that tended to be too full anyway.

This decision came around the time that my frozen wilderness life was beginning to thaw. I was finding that if I could manage to get alone and be with God then I could begin to sense him for myself – and this realisation made me feel parched and thirsty for his presence.

I didn't need any 'highs' at meetings – being alone with Jesus and experiencing the warmth, richness and sweetness of his closeness was more than enough for me. To my utter amazement, once my iciness had thawed, I could sense God's presence even more acutely than I had before. Perhaps three years of anaesthesia had sharpened my awareness.

I could see that in my forties I needed to set a pattern for the rest of my life and that it must give priority to time spent with God. That was fine in theory – in practice it was hard. Our children aged eighteen, twenty and twenty-two have half left home but are still half there. As young adults they need the liberty to make their own noise, have their own friends in, and not constantly be nagged by mother to do or not do this, that or the other. There were times when I felt as if my whole life had been invaded by them, their friends and above all their music. Each of them has his or her own stereo set in the bedroom and it penetrates every corner of the house – seemingly all the time! I found it totally impossible to pray with their noise coming at me from every direction – nor could I enforce silence for a set period without being so embarrassed that it wasn't worth the effort.

I could see that I needed to get alone to pray but I couldn't see how or when. Then one day, belting down the motor-way, racing from a convention back to the office, I could see that my daft racing had to stop. I had to make pools of quiet with God in my busy lifestyle if I was to survive and grow as a Christian.

'God, how can I make it possible?' I thought.

And then the garden shed flashed into mind. All down the M1 I thought about that shed, and the more I thought, the more my idea grasped me. Why didn't I turn the garden shed into a place to which I could escape?

I knew it would involve a lot of work, and I doubted that my husband would share my enthusiasm if he had to do *all* the work required. So, the following Saturday I tucked my husband up to sleep in for the morning, commandeered my youngest son and together we tackled the shed. Junk was thrown out or stored elsewhere, walls were scrubbed ready for white-washing, the cement floor was scrubbed for carpeting with the old kitchen carpet and I could see what that shed might be.

Over the weeks we put in electricity, struggled to make the shed watertight, and had fun making up DIY kits of office furniture.

The result? The result is far more valuable than a mere garden shed could ever be. It is now a place where I can escape and be alone with God. It is private and can be locked – so no one wanders in and catches me praying, and I am saved from my own or their embarrassment. Because the shed is made of brick, sound is muffled outside and so I can play worship tapes to my heart's content without annoying anyone. It is curtained and so I can draw the curtains and shut myself away unobserved. If I want to worship God with my hands, arms, legs, feet then no one is there to catch me and make me self-conscious or awkward. I can pray aloud or silently. It can be just me and God – the two of us alone, and this is something my soul needs.

It is now six years since my fortieth birthday, and I have emerged from the years following that day with a secure knowledge that God is able to keep me from falling when I cannot keep myself; that he restores the sense of his presence when he sees it is right to do so; and that it is safe to go on walking and trusting him even when he seems to be far away.

For me, coming out has been accompanied by the ability to sense God in a deeper way than before. But I have found that intercessory prayer is not quite as straightforward as it used to be when I was younger. I am no longer quite so confident that I am always so clear about what God wants to do in a person's life that I can ask definitely and specifically.

I used to think that praying in faith was asking God to do what I knew he wanted to do. Having been a Christian now for thirty years, I have come to see that God's ways are not my ways – I may think I know what is God's best for someone but I sometimes find I'm wrong! I didn't know after all, and God used means other than those I have asked him to use, to achieve the end he desired in someone's life.

Therefore, it's rare that I confidently and honestly pray, 'Lord, give Mary that job please!' because I don't know whether, in God's long term economy, that job is going to be the best thing for Mary or not. Instead, I can offer Mary and her situation to God and silently hold her before God, trusting him to work out in her life that which is best for her.

I find it harder, not easier, to pray for families in massive need. How do you pray after watching families devastated by bombs in the Lebanon; floods wrecking homes and lands in Africa; boat people being raped, mutilated and drowned on the South China Seas? What can I say in prayer? Words cannot express my heart but I have learned that there are times when words are not necessary in prayer. I can come to God in my garden shed, and I can silently bring to him what I have been thinking about. I know that my pain is just a faint reflection of the pain his great fatherly heart feels when men are hurt so much. In silent prayer I can enter into God's pain for the suffering of the world. I can inarticulately try to let God's Holy Spirit pray through me, that God's will shall be done on earth – that the broken shall be mended; the hurt healed; injustice righted; the oppressed set free; and the widows and fatherless provided for.

I find it helpful to try to visualise the person or situation for whom I'm praying, and mentally lift them to God and hand them into his hands for him to hold and care for them. Silently and wordlessly I try to focus all my attention and energy on to this – to mentally give that person or situation to God. This is hard work – it takes effort and concentration, but for me it is now what intercessory prayer often involves.

This way of praying has begun to open me up to God far more than before. In some ways praying like this means that God is more able to speak to me if he wants to. In the past God used to speak to me through his word, the Bible. He still does of course, but he also sometimes sows seed thoughts into my mind as I bring people and situations to him in prayer . . . and sometimes those seed thoughts result in my being in part the answer to my own prayers!

For me, middle-aged spirituality has become something that is rather different from the adolescent spirituality I first experienced when I became a Christian at fourteen. This older, wiser and more mature faith is far richer – and is something I have proved stands the test of life at its toughest. I have been through a spiritual wilderness experience, and have come out the other side with the joyous, liberating knowledge that God *is* good and the longer you follow him the richer life becomes.

Clive Calver

Prayer to the God Who is There

Clive Calver was born and brought up near Ipswich in Suffolk. He spent his teenage years in north London.

After graduating from London Bible College, he spent eleven years as a full-time evangelist and Bible teacher. He worked from 1975–82 as National Director of British Youth for Christ and then spent a year as Programme Director of Mission England. In the spring of 1983 he was appointed General Secretary of the Evangelical Alliance.

Clive has continued his involvement with British Youth for Christ as Vice-President. He is a Governor of Moorlands Bible College, and serves on the Federal Board of Mission England and the Executive Committee of Mission to London. He is the author of several books and serves as one of the leaders of Milton Keynes Free Church.

Clive is thirty-five, married to Ruth and has four children: two girls (Vicky and Suzannah) and two boys (Kristen and Gavin). He enjoys golf, swimming and playing with the kids.

There is nothing – but nothing – which amazes me more about God than the manner in which he answers prayer.

The idea of God as a super-being, imposing his will on mankind, is one which I find perfectly comprehensible. But God as a Father hearing the cries of his children – disciplining, correcting and answering – with time for each one of us – that I find truly amazing!

Having accepted that as fact, I find it hard to doubt that he will ever fail to provide for his children. The divine response to our requests may often not be what we would wish for, but it is not in the character of God to fail to reply!

It was 1972. Ruth and I were due to be married. I had faced up to the stern parental question of whether I could keep their daughter in the manner to which she had grown accustomed. My answers must have seemed very unsatisfactory. The tax-man was dissatisfied too. After all, my taxable income had amounted to less than £120 for the previous year. I could earn five times that amount and still not pay a penny in taxation.

But Ruth's parents had been involved in Christian service for over thirty years; they knew only too well that marriage to a young evangelist would not provide material security in the world's terms.

There really was not much time before the wedding and we still had no home in which to start our married lives. We could have had a room with either set of parents, but somehow that solution didn't seem right. So we prayed.

A couple of weeks before the wedding day God gave his answer – half a house in South London, rent free, for a year, given by a non-Christian we had never met: I was, quite honestly, speechless. I knew in theory that God answers prayer, but this exceeded my wildest dreams. Friends encouraged us to understand that if we served God faithfully then he would not, could not, ever let us down.

Unbeknown to the two of us, the best was yet to come! The one year period was nearly up. Prayer was approaching desperation because I still had not learned this basic lesson. One day I felt strangely constrained, while driving up the M6, to turn off and visit a married couple, teachers with whom I had once stayed for a fortnight when I was part of a mission team in the area.

This couple were exceptionally pleased to see me. I couldn't understand their enthusiasm until they shared their story.

God had clearly called them to serve him as missionaries in West Africa with Wycliffe Bible Translators. The problem they faced was what to do with their house, furniture, and wedding presents. Common sense dictated selective selling. But when they prayed, it became apparent that such action was not in God's scheme of things for them.

Following his instructions, having offered the house to both sets of parents, they wanted to see Ruth and me so that they could give their house, furniture and wedding presents to us. As a gift! It is not surprising that when they then went to Bible College and five days before term started had nowhere to live, parental concern overspilled. A visit was arranged by one set of parents. People prayed. Before term started a house was provided for this couple. It was in the countryside, but near the college, the rent was eight pounds a week and the house came complete with swimming pool and tennis court in the grounds! The parents were amazed, but reassured. Now, after several years of missionary service, that couple can witness to a series of answered prayers. Not least is related to the fact that they were reluctantly childless. It is scarcely surprising that, in view of their openness to sacrifice for the Lord, he reversed the natural order for them, and today they have two lovely children.

Furthermore, Ruth and I can never forget that all we own is a gift from God, through his people, by prayer.

It is that recognition which is so important for today. God is not seated in the heavenlies, benevolently looking down on us as we gain psychological relief for our tensions through prayer. He is looking for a praying people in order that he may hear and answer prayer. That does not give us a licence to draw up our own shopping lists at all times, but it does introduce us to a Lord who deeply cares for his people.

The Heart of the Matter

Four thousand people were crammed into the Big Top. But nobody spoke a word. The call had come, loud and clear, to be quiet before God. No one moved.

I believe that we can be too casual, too comfortable in prayer. There comes a time when God can move from being a benign Grandad and be reduced in our minds to the level of just a celestial chum. As John White writes in *People in Prayer*, 'We may be striving for honesty, openness, a break from ritual, stereotype and so on, all of which are good. Conversational prayer, for instance, can be a breakthrough for some people. But because we are human, we are tone deaf to awe.'

I wish I could point to great personal devotion in my prayer life, or to heights of lofty eloquence, or to a daily discipline of several hours on my knees. Of course there have been times of jubilation in heavenly places, periods of intercession; but they have not occupied the paramount place in my own prayer life. That would be more straight-forwardly described as a stumbling approach towards the living God.

In fact, any fluency in words that I might possess dries up before him. My testimony in prayer is reduced to a simple phrase – I called, and he answered. You see, those desperate shouts from lives committed to Jesus are the stuff of which answered prayer is made!

Along with so many others, my first memories of prayer lie in a few recited words on my knees by my bed at around five years of age. A year later, as a somewhat precocious, and not very sweet and innocent six year old, I was given some verses to recite at a Sunday School anniversary. I stood there in my grey jacket and short trousers in a little village chapel and proclaimed:

> I often say my prayers,
> But do I ever pray?
> And does the meaning of my heart
> Go in the words I say.
>
> I may as well kneel down
> And worship gods of stone;
> As offer to the living God
> A prayer of words alone.
>
> For words without the heart
> The Lord will never hear;
> Nor will he to those lips attend
> Whose thoughts are not sincere.

Talk about 'out of the mouths of babes and sucklings'! For those words remain as true today as they have ever been.

I still find it hard to accept that sincerity is an adequate substitute for personal innocence in approaching the living God, to recognise that all my failures, faults and weaknesses are covered by the blood of Jesus Christ and that I can speak to the God who made me. Yet such are the facts of the matter. Ever since I cried out to him as a nineteen-year-old in the East End of London for forgiveness and reconciliation to himself, I have experienced a God who is in the listening business!

A few years ago I was touring across Canada with a Christian music group. We were in two large vans. We had preaching engagements in all the major cities, and often had to drive through the night to get from one place to the next.

One night I was travelling in the second van. We were trailing the first van, at midnight, on a long, open road. The miles slipped by. Then suddenly the night lit up with a flash! I was sitting in the front passenger seat, next to the driver, so had a grandstand view of all that followed.

The fuel pipe in the forward van had fractured and petrol was spilling on to the road. The pipe itself had fallen downwards and was now being dragged along the road, lighting up the night with the sparks it created. We knew that the other van had a full tank of petrol and that our friends, both married men, were a second away from eternity. We prayed urgently while our driver desperately tried to gain the attention of the other vehicle, flashing his lights over and over again because he had discovered that his horn was out of order. More and more petrol gushed onto the road and into the sparks. Still we prayed.

It seemed an eternity, it must have been all of a minute, before we persuaded the van ahead to stop. When the friends in it got out and saw what had happened they instantly dived into the ditch at the roadside.

It would be no surprise for you to discover that we held a prayer-time of thanksgiving that night for the way in which the living God had once again reversed the natural order of things for just a few moments in order to deliver his people from disaster. The fact that God answers prayer is never something which we are at liberty to take for granted. Always we should return to say 'thank you'. Such gratitude will rarely be demure, polite and low-key. 'One of them, when he saw he was healed, came back, praising God in a *loud voice*. He threw himself at Jesus' feet and thanked him' (Luke 17.15–16, italics mine). It's a real pity about the other nine who never had time to return into the release of giving thanks!

Not Turned On, but Plugged In!
Genuine prayer can never just be turned on and off like a tap. I have had to discover that the living God will not meekly fall into my agenda; I must learn to respond to his. It is never enough to make our own plans and then ask him to bless and honour them – instead we have to discover his will and fall into line with that!

When we pray we need first to find forgiveness because,

'Your iniquities have separated you from your God' (Isaiah 59.2) and the road back begins when we count the cost and turn back to the Lord Jesus for restoration and cleansing. Our hidden sins and stubborn wills have to be dealt with before God will listen. Only then will we realise that God will not fall in with *our* way for our lives, but we must comply with *his*! 'I know, O Lord, that a man's life is not his own; it is not for man to direct his steps. Correct me, Lord' (Jeremiah 10.23–24).

If we fail to learn to listen to God we could end up running our lives according to our own human understanding. That is a sure recipe for disaster! Through listening prayer, and voluntary submission to God's will, he can tell us all that we need to know.

Then, when we are asked, 'What is it you want?' (Nehemiah 2.4) we can respond in the same terms of confident assertion with which Nehemiah could reply to the king. We know that we can convey the will of God, not just the tyranny of our own good ideas.

Such familiarity with the will of God comes through the practice of being in his presence. It may sound legalistic, but I am convinced that we do need to be disciplined in order to pray with maximum effectiveness. Very few of us feel a naturally genuine enthusiasm for daily prayer without first building up the habit. I know of no shortcuts or easy answers!

Nowadays some of us fail to see our prayers answered in the affirmative because we are content to pray as *we* think best; then for safety's sake we add, 'If it be the Lord's will'. We use those words as a spiritual escape route so that we can justify general, rather than specific prayer. That way we avoid taking risks!

Early in our married lives God placed Ruth and me in a situation that broke through that barrier. I had gone off to minister in Tyneside, we weren't on the phone at home, and I had not realised that there was no money in the bank (and certainly no overdraft arrangement!). Ruth was at home with ten pence in her purse, almost no food in the larder and I was not due back for ten days.

She turned to prayer. She had to. There was no room for escape routes. She simply asked God to provide for her and went to bed confident that a cheque would arrive from somewhere in the morning's post. Next morning, no cheque, nor the next, nor the next. Nine mornings came and went before the Lord allowed a cheque to come through. But each day, without her mentioning her needs to anyone, Ruth received all that she needed: transport to and from college, invitations to meals, food on the doorstep, as God demonstrated in a very simple way that specific prayer brings a specific answer – not necessarily the answer we would have made, but certainly his! Ten days later Ruth still had her ten pence, but she also had a story to tell of a Father who loves to answer the prayers of his children.

James demanded believing prayer: 'If it is the Lord's will' (James 4.15). But he goes on to say: 'Is any one of you sick? He should call the elders of the church to pray over him and anoint him with oil in the name of the Lord. And that prayer offered in faith will make the sick person well' (James 5.14–15). The implication here is that we will seek to ascertain the will and purpose of God before we pray, not afterwards! Otherwise all we are doing is conveniently sweeping under the carpet what for some of us could be a vast array of generalised unanswered prayer.

Why did Jesus always obtain positive answers? 'Father, I thank you that you have heard me. I know that you always hear me' (John 11.41–42). A stupendous claim, which was immediately supported by the resurrection of Lazarus from the dead! Jesus' secret was quite straightforward. He lived in such close proximity to his Father that he always knew the will of God *before* he prayed.

The same can be true for believers today. We also can obediently listen for God's will and in submission to that will can pray along those lines, as instructed. In that way Jesus' words are fulfilled, 'You may ask me for anything in my name, and I will do it' (John 14.14).

John loved Jesus, and out of that relationship he learned enough to be able to write, 'This is the assurance we have in approaching God: that if we ask anything according to his will, he hears us. And if we know that he hears us – whatever we ask – we know that we have what we asked of him' (1 John 5.14–15).

Although *we* do the praying, it is actually God himself who initiates prayer. He uses us as his hands and feet on the earth, but also as his heart and mouthpiece. We respond to his prompting by interceding in the direction which he has revealed to us. Now this is quite different to the usual practice in prayer of just diving in, then praying somewhat haphazardly for whatever comes into our heads at the time.

This concept of strategic prayer is vital to an evangelist. After all where would we be without the evidence of answered prayer to use as sermon illustrations! On a more serious note, what I am really trying to get across is this – we should first pray what to pray about – and then get on with it!

Moving On

When John encourages us into the prayer of faith he is merely being consistent with the life of Jesus. He uniquely set the pattern of a life lived by faith, and clearly demonstrated the difference between faith and foolishness. He always sought to find out his Father's will and then acted on that. If we expect God always to honour and agree to all our own ideas then that is mere foolishness, for we are playing at being God. In contrast, faith is understanding the will of God and having unshakable confidence that, against all odds, he will bring his purposes to pass.

The joy then comes in passing on our experiences of faith in order that we might build up the faith of others. It is quite easy to generate the attitude that if God will do it for them, he may well answer prayer for me. Such faith building will prepare a people who believe God for all that he will do among them.

The means by which God answers prayer will vary. Usually he will use his people to fulfil his purposes. But if ignorance, disobedience, deafness on the part of Christians intrudes, an alternative plan on God's part is used and nothing actually prevents God's plan from moving on.

Some four years ago I was working with Youth for Christ. My assistant there was a young Oxford graduate named Mike Morris. When we gained a secretary, Mike didn't ask any questions. He simply ordered an electric golfball typewriter, which in those days cost around six hundred pounds, and started to pray for the money. He had felt quite certain that this was right and necessary and I felt quite happy to support his act of faith.

The typewriter duly arrived. So did the bill. But not the money! Prayers seemed to go unanswered until one night, when the bill was due for payment, I was driving up the M1 with Mike. We stopped at the Rothersthorpe Service Area. I rejoined Mike after he had filled the car with petrol. Further up the motorway he revealed that in the service area he had noticed a ten pound note on the floor, then another, and another, finally a whole bundle of them. Mike had not reported his find (which proved to be exactly six hundred pounds), feeling that it would be better to surrender the find at a police station.

The next morning surprised police officers confirmed that if the find went unclaimed for a month the money was Mike's and that Youth for Christ could hold it on their behalf for the interim period. The find was unclaimed and to this day I don't know whose, presumably ill-gotten, gains the Lord diverted – but I do know that nothing prevents him answering prayer.

Meditation, intercession, thanksgiving, petition – all these are vital subjects in prayer. All need to be experienced in our lives. Yet at the end of the day we need to affirm, both to one another, and to the world at large, that our God reigns and acts out that reign on the stage of human history.

Some will sniff, and speak of triumphalism. Yet I firmly believe that we have significantly failed in this century to confidently proclaim the deeds of our God: to affirm that prayer is no mere going through the motions but communicating with a God who acts in power; to assert to those who whisper about the cheap tricks from the enemy that 'they ain't seen nuthin' yet'.

During Mission England, as believing prayer was focused by God's people on those who had never met the Lord, it was tremendous to see people being prayed into the Kingdom of God. What made the difference – as thousands of new prayer triplets and prayer groups emerged – was a new sense of confidence that God is at work among his people today: doing great things.

As Elijah challenged the prophets of Baal and Asherah all those years ago, ' "Then you call on the name of your god, and I will call on the name of the Lord. The god who answers by fire – he is God." . . . Then the fire of the Lord fell . . . When all the people saw this, they fell prostrate and cried, "The Lord – he is God! The Lord – he is God!" ' (1 Kings 18.24,38,39).

The truth is that our God answers prayer!